# Driving the EU Forward
## Straight Talks with Maroš Šefčovič

GW00802464

## About the author

Maroš Šefčovič is the Vice-President of the European Commission responsible for inter-institutional relations and administration (2009-2014). Previously, he was Slovakia's Permanent Representative to the EU and Ambassador to Israel. He was recently a lead candidate in the 2014 European elections in Slovakia.

*Mr Šefčovič writes in a personal capacity and his views do not necessarily reflect those of the European Commission.*

DRIVING THE EU FORWARD

# STRAIGHT TALKS WITH MAROŠ ŠEFČOVIČ

JOHN HARPER PUBLISHING

Published by John Harper Publishing
27 Palace Gates Road
London N22 7BW, United Kingdom.

www.johnharperpublishing.co.uk

Distributed by Turpin Distribution Services Ltd.

Driving the EU Forward – Straight Talks with Maroš Šefčovič

ISBN 978-0-9571501-7-1

Typeset in 10pt/ 12pt. Palatino

Printed and bound in the EU at the Gutenberg Press, Malta.

www.howtheEUworks.com

# TABLE OF CONTENTS

# ACKNOWLEDGMENTS

I would like to express my especial thanks to Manuel Szapiro, for without his skills and perseverance in pulling the text into shape this book would have struggled to see the light of day. His ability to cope with the demanding schedules and unsocial hours of a Commissioner made all the difference.

This also applies to the other close members of my team whose hard work and motivation have, under the talented and reliable leadership of my Head of Cabinet Juraj Nociar, made a world of difference during my term as European Commissioner for inter-institutional relations and administration.

I am indebted to all of them and to the Commission services, with which we worked in close and fruitful cooperation throughout this mandate in delivering on important files for our fellow EU citizens, for their elected representatives and for our committed EU staff.

# PROLOGUE

## Why this book?

To be at the heart of the European Commission, with a chance to shape the future of our continent, is exciting. And, at times, frustrating.

One of the most frequent criticisms of the EU is that it is remote and out-of-touch with the realities of citizens' everyday lives, that decisions are taken in 'Brussels' with little or no perceived democratic link or accountability.

As Commissioner in charge of administration and inter-institutional relations, I have taken a number of initiatives to boost both representative democracy, through greater parliamentary oversight and participatory democracy, via the strengthened involvement of citizens in setting the EU agenda.

But very early on I also came to realise how difficult it is for the vast majority of our fellow citizens, those with no direct contact with the EU institutions, to understand how the EU functions, and how they can relate to it.

Part of my daily work as a European Commissioner consists of giving 'straight talks' to a wide range of audiences – including students, journalists, NGOs, parliamentarians and government officials – explaining what it is I do as a Commissioner and how the EU impacts their lives. But people expect more – and quite rightly so. They need to know what can be done for and, most importantly, by them. They need to take ownership of the EU project.

The EU system is complex and therefore easily misrepresented by populist parties and some of the media alike. This complexity can sometimes act as a deterrent to citizens. But this complexity need not be an insurmountable obstacle, if the mechanisms are clearly explained and the purpose of EU policy discussed more extensively and collectively owned.

I am hoping that this book will help people understand how the EU works, what has been achieved, the main challenges ahead of us and – most importantly of all – what can and should be done to reconnect the EU with the people of Europe.

## Why now?

We are at a pivotal point in time, where the involvement of citizens is more than ever key to the successful development of the EU. 2014 is a year of changes. In the months leading up to the European Parliament elections, EU politics and the EU project have become hot topics. For the first time, the issue of the relationship between the results of the elections and the choice of the next President of the Commission has been on the agenda, with each European-level political party putting forward a lead 'candidate' for the presidential role. While this relationship is, at the time of writing, a 'work in progress', there can be no doubt that the rules of the game are changing, and in the direction of more democratic accountability.

All this can help move us away from the perception of a 'bureaucratic' type of European integration, to a more 'democratic' type. But this comes with a condition. Our fellow citizens need clear political alternatives to be offered to them. Pro-European forces must show distinctly and distinctively what it is they offer their electorates. They need to show in particular how their respective programmes can provide a response to the economic and social situation which is causing great distress to many in the Member States.

For we simply cannot afford to let Eurosceptic or, even worse, anti-European parties dictate the political narrative. I say this because in the last few years I have witnessed that there are fewer political leaders actually engaging – even critically – in the defence of the EU project, however it may be defined.

We are risking a lot more than we may imagine: younger generations are not necessarily fully aware of the dark chapters we have closed thanks to EU integration – world wars, hatreds between nations, state-sponsored racism, anti-semitism, totalitarianism, fascism and genocide. I say this very deliberately: if we don't watch out in these turbulent times, anti-European forces could well take us back to the darkest hours of protectionism and nationalism and, as a result, to a weaker, less progressive, less tolerant and less free Europe. That Europe, I can tell you, is still fresh in the minds of people like me who – little more than two decades ago – were living behind the Iron Curtain. I shall come back to that experience later on in the book.

I must add, also, that in looking at the options ahead of us we should always take into consideration the 'cost of non-Europe'. And I say this because we don't necessarily make this salutary 'mind switch'. What would we do for instance, what price would we and our companies have to pay, if our goods could not circulate freely in our 500-million strong market? How would we react if we could not travel, study, work or settle in other EU countries, if we had to endure border controls again? What if we had to change currencies each time we went to a different Eurozone country (with a strict limit as to how much money we could take with us)? And if we had to resort – as in the past – to endless battles of competitive devaluations between our national currencies and experience soaring (imported) inflation as a result? And these are but a few examples…

## The European elections, and beyond

With this in mind, pro-EU forces must take the lead. There is no alternative. Not just as a 'one-off' in the 2014 European Parliament elections, but in political campaigning in all our countries in the months and years to come, we need to speak up for the actual and potential achievements of our collective efforts, the successes achieved together, the relevance of the EU to the lives of each and every citizen, the ways to involve people further (directly or indirectly) in the decision-making – and we must offer solutions as to what should be changed or improved in the near future. Our message to EU citizens should be clear: we are working for and with you. And we need to do more still. We need to show that the EU is able to respond to our citizens' concerns, and that their votes do matter; we need to demonstrate that they can have an impact on the future, depending on who they choose to represent them.

Through these 2014 European elections – with parties for the first time putting up candidates for the post of President of the Commission and with future Commissioners themselves standing for election (all of this thanks to sheer democratic pressure going beyond Treaty requirements!); through members of the College being designated by the people's representatives; and beyond 2014, through national, regional and local elections and the participation of these representatives in EU policy-making, at all levels of democracy, we can work together towards a more democratic and political union.

This book is intended as a modest but engaged contribution to this debate, based on the 'straight talks' I have had with a range of audiences inside and – mostly – outside the Commission, and on looking back at what a five-year term at the helm of the EU has taught me. In this book I want to propose the thread of a positive agenda to drive the EU forward, in order to restore jobs, growth, citizens' involvement and much-needed confidence and pride in our continent.

# 1. THE EUROPEAN COMMISSION : LIFE FROM THE INSIDE

The Commission is often seen as a remote institution. Many people ask me with a degree of bewilderment, 'what do you actually do in Brussels?', and 'all these Commission staff, what do we really need them for?'

## An undeservedly unpopular institution

Going to hearings before national parliaments is always a very interesting exercise. As Commissioner responsible, amongst other things, for relations with national parliaments I undertook to visit them all at least once (some, several times) during my mandate, to discuss ways to get them better involved in EU policy-making. I have listened to MPs and tried to account for the actions taken by the Commission across the board.

I will come back later to the importance I have given to the 'political dialogue' with national parliaments which was initiated under President Barroso. For now, let me tell you a short anecdote. During one of these – most often generally very constructive meetings – I was directly confronted by a rather Eurosceptic party leader (of the sort who can be found of course in both national parliaments and the European Parliament).

His intervention was roughly as follows:

> You call yourself a 'Commissioner'… But tell me Mr Šefčovič – who has 'commissioned' you to interfere with our lives? You come here and will surely tell us what our national budget should look like, what taxes we should pay, what employment benefits or pensions we should receive, what environmental policy we should pursue. How on earth can someone like you, living in Brussels, whom my constituents have never voted for, get to decide what budget should be spent and social benefits should be earned? This is solely the realm of national sovereignty and it should stay that way.

I was not in fact really coming before my critic's parliament to lecture its honourable members about their national budget – indeed a matter of national sovereignty. I was rather coming to present the Commission's general economic orientations and our country-specific guidance (with recommendations on economic policy and structural reforms) and – most importantly – to hear the MPs' views before discussions took place with national governments and decisions were taken by all of them collectively in the Council.

However, it was in a way immaterial whether what my critic was saying was 'wrong' or not. I actually did understand where part of his complaint was coming from. Before I joined the Commission I myself had only seen it from the outside. As an outsider, it did look to me as a product of the EU's own internal logic, certainly not the emanation of the democratically expressed will of its citizens.

My experience from within the Commission has shed a different light on things. So let me share some related thoughts with you.

First, the Commission is a *political* body, even if it also relies on a solid administration. Whether people like it or not, it is not a purely technocratic institution. It possesses political, democratic legitimacy. Let me expand.

The Commission has to be endorsed by the directly elected European Parliament. Its President is nowadays proposed by the Heads of State and Government of the Member States '*taking into account the results of European Parliament elections*' and is '*elected*' – both terms used by the EU Treaty – by the European Parliament. The College of Commissioners is also approved by both the elected members of the European Parliament and our Heads of State and Government. Not enough? In 2014 the European political parties have put forward 'candidates' for the Commission presidency. The process of appointing the Commission President, traditionally opaque and dominated by a few big Member State governments, is moving towards one that is more open and democratic – a trend which shows the determination to bring the EU closer to its citizens. Once the European Parliament is elected, the choice of President will still very much depend on political groups coalition-building inside the European Parliament. It will also directly involve the Heads of State and Government (themselves democratically elected) in the European Council. Its President, Herman Van Rompuy, has already taken the initiative of convening a summit in the immediate aftermath of the elections, just two days after, to have the EU Heads of State and Government discuss the outcome. At the time of writing this is 'work in progress'. What is for sure: both now and in the future, we can expect plenty of 'creative tension' between the European Council and the European Parliament – but it is after all through such creative tension and 'balance of powers' that democracy lays ever firmer foundations.

Once the President is elected, the Commissioners are proposed by the elected national governments of the EU. And it is up to each designated Commissioner to prove his or her worth to the European Parliament. To this end, we have to go through a Congress-style confirmation hearing before parliamentary committees dealing with our proposed portfolio. These committees are made up of elected parliamentarians who are real specialists in the subject at hand, and they decide whether we are up for the job. So these hearings are rather like several-hour oral entrance exams.

We actually refer to these hearings as 'grillings'. And this – I must say – is no exaggeration. For the post of Commissioner in charge of inter-institutional relations and administration, I had to go through nearly four hours of such oral interviews, with questions flying at me from all across the room, and a maximum of two minutes to respond to each one of them (the microphone is cut off to prevent long-winded 'waffle'…). I experienced at first hand the high level of expertise and close scrutiny of the MEPs, who were looking for strong EU commitment, but also deep interest, knowledge of, and well-grounded strategic orientations for the proposed portfolio. Yes, of course there are also some political manoeuvres going on. As prospective Commissioners, we need to prepare these hearings rigorously so as to master the substance and build up some political support beforehand. Our language skills are also severely tested during these interviews. It is no easy ride, believe me: it reminded me of those defining moments in life, those 'rites of passage' like the final exams at high school or university – the stress, the pressure mounting, the expectations… At the end, once I had gone through these 'grillings', I was made aware of the fact that the members present in the Constitutional Affairs committee (AFCO) had unanimously agreed that I was fit-for-the-job. That came as a relief.

Once in office, finally, the College continues to answer to the elected European Parliament which can dismiss it at any time. The European Parliament skilfully uses all the instruments at its disposal to make the Commission accountable for its work: through hearings of Commissioners, the setting up of committees of inquiry, oral and written questions (13,500 per year according to the latest statistics), the 'structured dialogue' with all specialised committees leading up to the presentation in plenary of the Commission's work programme, the discussions on the Commission's legislative proposals, the adoption of amendments and own-initiative reports (e.g. asking the Commission to present a proposal), the negotiations on the EU draft budget, etc. The persistent democratic tension between the Commission and the European Parliament is quite similar, if not identical, to that encountered in our national parliamentary democracies.

In any case, to come back to our Eurosceptic friend's argument: if one looks a bit closer at how the EU functions, the Commission does not exactly appear as a purely bureaucratic institution…

Second, *the Commission is not some all-powerful body*. As a Commissioner I actually can hardly decide anything on my own (as opposed to collectively, together with all my fellow Commissioners). And when the College of Commissioners adopts a position, we then submit nearly all our initiatives to the elected ministers and members of the European Parliament who together are the ultimate decision-makers. Hence on draft national budgetary plans the Commission merely gives its *opinion*. And on national reform programmes we issue draft *recommendations* that need Member States' endorsement. Even if we are to propose a sanction (or fine) – for example, in the case of an excessive national budget deficit, this has to go to the Council who can oppose it, and it can only be done once the ministers have established that there is a strong case for it in the country under review. So if some national leaders make it seem that decisions are taken unknowingly (or unwittingly), even in areas where surveillance has recently been strengthened, this is simply not true! Decisions are made *in* Brussels, but not *by* Brussels. They are made by the citizens' elected national and European representatives who remain – and should be held – democratically accountable for them.

Third, *Member States remain competent in many areas of sovereignty*, notably as far as fiscal, social, employment, education and cultural policies are concerned. The pooling of sovereignty is very limited in these policy areas. In these fields of limited transfer, financial support and benchmark cooperation can, however, prove extremely beneficial. Take, as examples, the mobility of students with the Erasmus programme which has already benefited more than 3 million students in the EU, the 'youth guarantee' (partly financed by the European Social Fund) to ensure all young people in Europe receive a decent offer within four months of leaving formal education or becoming unemployed, or the Media programme which contributes to the development of European film and audio-visual industry.

All this being said, the fact of the matter is that there is currently very little shared 'ownership' by the European public of decisions taken on their behalf in Brussels. The EU institutions, like national ones, are at the service of their citizens. But when do we hear the citizens refer to the Commission as 'our Commission', or the European Parliament as 'our Parliament' or the EU Council as 'our Council'? Not often, to say the least! This needs to be remedied.

So, how can we make sure that the citizens relate to the decisions taken by their representatives in Brussels (or as a matter fact Strasbourg)?

Let me mention three elements that I have seen to be particularly relevant during my term as Commissioner:

First, the *communication* issue. Basically the communication chain is broken: some national leaders simply do not assume responsibility vis-à-vis their national constituencies for the decisions they themselves take in Brussels. There lies the weakest link! And it accounts for a misleading perception of the EU – or rather a conveniently insulated, dissociated and hostile 'Brussels' – taking the blame for all the hardship endured by citizens, and seen as interfering with people's wellbeing and the welfare state. The mass media, including social media, also play a crucial role in communicating EU decisions to the citizens – the way they are taken, their motivation and impacts. Politicians need to reflect on how they can best get across to the media what are at times complex and consensus based EU issues so as to ensure their coverage of EU affairs is enhanced in quantity and quality.

Second, the *democratic channels*. Accountability mechanisms should be reinforced at all levels (local, regional, national and EU) and in all their forms (representation and participation). The EU is not only about what happens in Brussels and not only an elite project. During my mandate, I've worked extensively on involving both citizens and parliaments better in EU policy making. But still more can be done – in particular to give a greater say to the European and national parliaments in the new EU economic governance framework. In view of the new shared responsibilities of the European Commission in the area of economic governance, it is important that a number of Commissioners benefit from democratic legitimacy via European Parliament elections. I am therefore hoping that in the next Commission we will have the highest number of Commissioners who have been 'elected' in this way!

Third, *joint action* – and *results*. We are all in the same boat. Not only the EU but all institutions – first amongst which are national ones – have suffered a sharp decline in public trust in the last six years. Suffice it to mention the Eurobarometer opinion surveys: trust in national governments decreased continuously from 41% to a record-low 23% over the period September 2007 to August 2013 while trust in the Commission fell from 52% to 36% over the same period. This cannot become a race to the bottom. What is at stake is the confidence and trust (or rather increasing lack of it) of the general public in political action. This is especially so in relation to the economic crisis which is causing great hardship among our citizens and putting political bonds under stress. We need to work together in providing tangible results to the people. The options to restore job-rich growth need to be discussed thoroughly in the framework of the results of the European Parliament elections.

## The College of Commissioners

What do I respond when I get asked what it's like to live and work in the Brussels 'bubble', distant from the realities of the Member States and their citizens?

On a humorous note: living in Brussels is good. The weather is not so great – granted (so you are actually not often distracted, and can work longer hours!), but the cuisine is quite something. As we like to say: 'German quantities combined with French quality'. And of course some 1,500 varieties of beer and the world renowned chocolate… As President Barrack Obama recently pointed out in his recent keynote speech in Brussels: 'it's easy to love a country famous for chocolate and beer'.

But, joking and clichés aside: most people in the Commission live far from their country of origin – their original home. And it is definitely not easy for them to leave, perhaps with their partner and children, the warmth of the South of Europe, the calm and transparency of the North, the generosity and spontaneity of Central and Eastern Europe. They leave behind their hometown, their family, their friends, their close networks… people that they will miss. They do so because they want to work for Europe, not primarily because they want to live and work in Brussels (or Luxembourg).

In doing so, and despite all of this, none of them loses touch with his or her roots. Those connections remain. Therefore, I cannot agree that the Commission works as (or in) a 'bubble'. *It is actually quite the opposite*: Commission staff and members of the College come from all countries of the EU and bring their different cultures with them. My fellow Commissioners know their countries of origin very well. They have all had important roles at national level before joining the Commission. Many of them are career politicians. And they travel back and forth to their country of origin – 'the country which they know best', in Commission parlance – very often, as well as to other EU countries. They do so to meet their respective governments, parliaments, businesses, civil society actors, social partners, students, the press, etc. This allows the College to adopt decisions with a profound knowledge of the realities back home. In addition all members of the College have an in-depth knowledge of their own portfolios and – on the principle of collegiality – are able to discuss those of their colleagues in our weekly meetings.

## How do we work? The weekly meetings with my fellow Commissioners

In the College room, we always sit in the same place. On my left, I was fortunate to sit next to Vice-President Neelie Kroes, in charge of the digital agenda. Neelie is a Dutch business-woman, very determined, to the point, frank, forceful, always stylish and elegant. When the College started she was the only member with a functioning twitter account (with already more than 20,000 followers) and, together with Kristalina Georgieva, to have a Facebook account. The other members of the College have followed suit!

It was always a pleasure to work with Neelie. Some readers may find this purely anecdotal, but I do remember some details very fondly: for instance, I always used to open her bottles of water in the meetings and we shared the excellent cappuccino (probably the best in Brussels) brought by her assistant ... this is simply good cooperation between Commissioners for you!

On my right I had at first sitting next to me Olli Rehn, our Finnish Commissioner in charge of the economic and monetary affairs portfolio. I remember going often through his notes and discussing with him the latest developments in relation to the economic crisis – this was of the utmost interest. He moved to the other side of the table when promoted to the post of Vice-President and in his seat came the Environment Commissioner Janez Potočnik, with whom we shared amongst other things a Sloven-ian-Slovakian sense of humour and a mutual passion for volley-ball and our children. All three members had participated in the previous College as respectively Competition, Enlargement and Research & Development Commissioners – so they definitely knew their way around in the Commission. They were, like my other colleagues, passionate members who strove to find practical solutions and were not afraid to speak their minds.

Discussions in the College meeting room are always open and frank. There is a great sense of companionship during our weekly College meetings. Of course we do not always agree but we work as a 'corps', with the EU interest at its heart.

You can easily imagine how difficult the discussions can be between Commissioners of different political backgrounds concerning measures to fight the crisis, on how to address the issue of austerity, on how to combine our energy and climate policies with our industry's strengthened competitiveness… but there is always a good spirit and final agreement is reached in a consensual way since we all have to defend it in public afterwards.

In this respect, I have always admired the patience and talent of the Commission's President, José Manuel Barroso, for proposing a solution that is acceptable to all Commissioners. He does this in full consciousness that the College is an EU microcosm, that we represent – in a way – the diversity of EU landscapes, that whatever gains the support of the College will be more likely to obtain support from the Member States in the Council and the European Parliament, with a much better chance to succeed and be adhered to by the citizens of Europe. Although according to the Commission rules of procedure the decision-making foresees simple majority, most decisions are therefore taken by consensus and the President of the Commission plays a big part in making this possible.

To enable Commissioners to be involved in the shaping of policy right from the start, President Barroso has introduced so-called 'orientation debates' early in the process. This enables the College to discuss a priority issue before proposals are actually prepared by the Commission services – addressing questions such as what shape the proposal should take, how to include an impact assessment, the timing, the likely political reactions, and later fine-tuning. We have had orientation debates on economic governance, the enlargement process, energy policy, climate change, industrial policy, etc., and this has allowed the political input to the discussion to be given at a much earlier stage than before.

In reaching agreement in the College, we always look very closely at the impact of our proposals on our Member States of origin, and on our citizens. We try our best to keep our feet on the ground – through the principle of 'smart regulation' (justifying why we are doing something), through contacts with our Member States' administrations, through rigorous and independent impact assessments, extensive consultations with stakeholders, and discussions on the 'added value' and substance of proposals. There are green papers to launch discussions on the 'whys and ifs', and white papers to discuss the 'hows', and there are subsidiarity and proportionality checks to justify not only the need to intervene at EU level but that this is the most effective and efficient option possible. For we know that our proposals will need to pass the 'reality tests' of the Council of Ministers and the European Parliament and – subsequently – that of their application on the ground. Our proposals have to be robust and well-grounded, with clearly justified added value, and anchored in the social, economic, environmental and political realities of a Union of 28 Member States.

And we – Commissioners – work on our initiatives with a medium to a long-term horizon, since we are less prone to the vicissitudes of electoral reshuffling than our counterparts in national governments. This means that we can try to make a difference over the five-year horizon that is given to us. In my period as Commissioner in charge of inter-institutional relations and administration, I managed, for instance, to (in no particular order):

– Get the European Citizens' Initiative – the first ever pan-European participatory democracy instrument – off the ground, so as to give citizens a direct voice in the shaping of EU policy making;

– Negotiate and implement an administrative reform to modernise the EU civil service and bring in substantial savings (around €5.8 billion extra over the period 2014-2020);

– Modernise the selection process for jobs in the EU institutions by using competence and computer-based testing – our new system now serves as a reference point or benchmark for many organisations in the world;

- Bring the Commission's strategic partnership with the European Parliament to the next level and beef up the political dialogue with national parliaments; this 'Lisbonisation' has greatly increased the parliamentary scrutiny of our work;

- Increase the Commission's transparency, thus allowing greater citizen access to consulted stakeholders, the work of expert groups, and of committees of Member States' representatives; and improving the transparency of lobbying activity through the setting up of a joint European Parliament – Commission transparency register, which already lists more than 6,500 organisations;

- Agree with the EU co-legislators (European Parliament and Council) on the first ever governance framework for all EU decentralised agencies;

- Reach an agreement with the EU co-legislators on a genuine legal statute for all EU political parties to enable them to carry out pan European campaigns in the future;

- Shape high-level discussions in the General Affairs Council (GAC) on such important horizontal issues as the economic crisis, the 7-year EU budget, and the accession of new Member States, and be part of the preparation of each European Council summit in the last five years – and we probably established some type of world record in the number of summits held to deal with the crisis! This was very often done with the involvement of Herman Van Rompuy, the European Council President, in our meetings.

All these achievements would have been very difficult – if not impossible – without a five-year political horizon.

## Are there too many Commissioners?

I quite often get told there are too many of us Commissioners by some of my counterparts in the Council!

And indeed we currently have one Commissioner per Member State. And, according to a European Council decision, this is bound to say that way.

But I cannot agree that there are too many Commissioners. I will tell you why: if you look at the structure of the Commission, the political leadership is actually very thin. At the political level, the Commission can only be represented by the Commissioners. There are no deputy ministers, state secretaries and the like of the sort to whom representation powers are traditionally delegated in national governments – and which sometimes results in executives of 30+ members. Coping with a much enlarged territory and increased competences, and facing the need to communicate more directly with national parliaments (notably with the opinions the Commission now issues on draft national budgets for Eurozone Member States), it is unlikely that a smaller College would be fit for purpose.

In addition, as I mentioned before, to perform our job properly we need to remain in touch with the realities of our 28 Member States. At the end of the day the Commission is like a microcosm of the EU at large and we need to make sure, when adopting decisions that pursue the EU interest, that these will be supported and implemented on the ground. The Commission is not working – in a bubble – for some stratospheric common good but for a pragmatic approach to problems.

Can you imagine, finally, if we had to adopt a very difficult decision affecting a particular country – for example, regarding fines to be applied over a merger, or national state aids, or closure of shipyards, or recommendations on national finances – without a Commissioner from that country participating in the College decision-making? How would that be perceived by public opinion in the affected country? It certainly would not help to bridge the gap with the citizens.

So Commissioners currently come from *all* the Member States. And they decide collectively. Thanks to collegiality we make sure that no Commissioner decides anything on his or her own. There is therefore no risk of capture of the entire decision-making process by a single pressure group or government.

## Our modern administration and its highly qualified staff

*Our staff – 'united in diversity'*

I have to say that throughout my mandate I've been most impressed by the quality – and diversity – of the staff working in the European Commission. It is a hard working and independent workforce which has to deal on a daily basis with the challenge of multicultural and multidisciplinary work.

Of course our rigorous selection process plays its part: in the past four years, the European Personnel Selection Office has processed over 300,000 candidates, out of which 4,000 became 'laureates', making them eligible for recruitment into the EU civil service. Through intense competency-based and multilingual assessment we ensure that only the very highest quality candidates are selected from across the whole continent.

I would like to highlight something that is not very well known (or has as a matter of fact been much researched). A recent independent study of the Commission (Hussein Kassim et al., *The European Commission of the Twenty-First Century*, Oxford University Press, 2013), showed that 96% of the staff joining the Commission came with prior work experience; only a handful joined straight after graduating. Newcomers thus bring the wealth and breadth of their prior experience, with a third actually being recruited from the private sector. And, contrary to a commonly held belief, the Commission workforce does not mainly consist of lawyers. This study shows that a much larger number of civil servants are actually scientists, economists or come from a business or political science background. In addition, EU staff are not uniformly federalist in their views. Quite the opposite: according to this research, EU staff hold an impressive range of beliefs on the EU (with not only federalists but also state-centrist views!). This diversity of nationalities, profiles and beliefs inside the Commission reflects the outside world. The Commission, and by extension the other EU institutions, are therefore a sort of landscape in miniature of the multicultural society in which we live. Civil servants (and others working for the EU) are reminded every day that their own working methods and ways of thinking are not the only valid ones. This daily transcending of cultural differences and languages is a great source of creativity inside the Commission. To me, European institutions and their multicultural staff epitomise the EU motto: 'united in diversity'.

Now on the numbers – always a sensitive issue. The number of staff in the Commission is around 33,000, which is not really so many considering the scale of the work they undertake. It is fewer than the size of an administration of a large city (Paris, Stockholm or Birmingham city councils, for example). If we take national comparisons, we find much higher figures, especially in big countries where a single government department can be several times bigger than the whole Commission, e.g. the UK Department of Work and Pensions which has 98,000 staff or the French Ministry of Agriculture with 40,000 people. Of course, it is true that their respective tasks are not strictly comparable… but, against that, the Commission does have to cover 28 Member States, with more than 500 million inhabitants, extending over nearly 4,500,000 sq. km; on top of this, it operates in three working languages (English, French and German) and needs to translate what it produces into the 24 EU official ones (DGT – our translation service – is actually the biggest Commission department with 2,500 staff). EU staff constantly need to adapt their work to the richness and administrative complexities of the entire Union, permanently dealing with the challenge of coming up with robust solutions that are workable in 28 diverse Member States.

In addition, EU personnel have seen new tasks steadily given to the EU institutions over the years, in particular to the European Commission – for instance in the areas of economic and budgetary surveillance, banking sector regulation and cybercrime. All this involves more work. In a context of budget constraints this has meant redeployment to priority tasks and an emphasis on exploiting IT tools to ensure value for money, efficiency and cost effectiveness.

Talking of which…

## The administration – providing better value-for-money for EU citizens

Some tabloids refer to the EU civil servant as – I quote – 'fat cats' whose working conditions and numbers have been left untouched by the crisis. This is simply untrue (in addition to insulting, of course).

As in the Member States, the conditions of EU staff have been adjusted to take account of budgetary austerity. Already in 2004, we had completely overhauled the Staff Regulations to adapt them to the needs of the enlarged EU (which went from 15 to 25 Member States in 2004, then 27 in 2007) and to principles of efficiency and cost effectiveness (according to so-called 'new public management' principles, derived from the private sector).

Ten years later, I reached an agreement with the European Parliament and the Council to push through wide-ranging reforms of the EU civil service and significantly drive down the cost of running the EU for each and every citizen. The context is the one we all know, marked by particularly difficult economic conditions across the EU, and with many national administrations having had to make significant reforms and cut costs as a result. It was only right that the European adminis-tration should also try to find savings, in the spirit of solidarity.

The objective was to adapt the Staff Regulations to a context of budget constraints and efficiency gains while keeping the EU civil service attractive and competitive. After long and sometimes difficult negotiations with EU staff unions and Member State governments alike, we were able to agree on measures to adjust the EU civil service to the new reality of doing better with less.

Amongst the measures which entered into force and were implemented during my mandate, I should mention:

– a 5% staff cut over five years;

– a four-year salary freeze;

– a 40-hour working week, one of the longest in European public administration (compared with e.g. 36 hours in the UK, 35 in France, 41 in Germany, 36 in the Netherlands, and 38 in Belgium), with no salary increase;

– a higher EU levy and a new career structure to reserve access to the best-paid jobs to the best performers;

– a pension reform including an increase of the retirement age to 66 (potentially 70), with a new link between pensions and life expectancy, as the Commission recommends for Member States, as well as a lower accrual rate;

– more extensive use of contract staff.

The first reform package will save €8 billion by 2020 and the second one €5.8 billion by 2020 on top of that, plus €1.5 billion per year in the long term.

But it is important to stress that these reforms have not led to a smaller workload for EU civil servants. On the contrary: the Member States continue to ask for ever more input from the Commission, with new tasks such as coordinating new eco-nomic governance measures (like assessing draft national budg-ets and drawing up national reform recommendations), creating a banking union, putting into motion the digital agenda, being the first on the spot to deliver humanitarian aid in case of national catastrophes, etc.

That's why I have also driven through major reforms of the way we work: restructuring services; creating support services shared by different departments; offering services to other EU institutions to benefit from efficiency gains; simplifying procedures; reviewing business processes; improving the IT infrastructure – all this is part of our day-to-day work to guarantee value for money.

The cost of running the EU was already very low – just 6% of the total EU budget is spent on day-to-day administration (salaries, pensions, buildings etc.), meaning the remaining 94% goes directly on policies and investments that benefit all EU citizens.

This 6% represents less than €16 per capita per year. In other words, the whole EU administration is working for €16 a year or 4 cents a day for each EU citizen. And, it's worth remembering that every year of this Commission the European Court of Auditors has found that that every single euro of the 6% is being properly spent, i.e. with no errors or mistakes – showing that even before my reforms the EU civil service offered extremely good value for money to European taxpayers.

As for the cost of EU policies (the remaining 94%), this money ultimately all goes back to EU citizens – in the form of subsidies for farmers, funding to the less well-off regions to create growth and jobs, grants for Erasmus students, assistance to researchers, support to young entrepreneurs, financing small and medium sized enterprises (SMEs), major energy, transport and ICT infrastructure projects, securing our own food supply, supporting mobility and employment services (via the Eures networks), encouraging youth employment schemes, providing enhanced consumer safety and passengers' rights, lower tariffs on roaming... and so on.

# 2. HOW HAS THE INSTITUTIONAL LANDSCAPE EVOLVED?

## How are decisions made?

EU legislation is always the outcome of a collective effort. EU institutions act as checks-and-balances on each other.
   In a nutshell, all EU legislation:

– is prepared by the Commission further to extensive and transparent consultations with stakeholders (on the basis of green and white papers) and with Member States, and as a result of robust assessments of its economic, social and environmental impact (including the impact on SMEs);
– has to be approved both by national ministers in the Council and by elected members of the European Parliament (and in practice most decisions are agreed upon by all ministers in the Council and a big majority in the European Parliament);
– is subject to national parliaments having the opportunity to react to each and every legislative proposal before it is formally discussed by the legislator – the Commission receives hundreds of such opinions every year and responds to each one of them.

## How do Member States operate in the Council?

A very important coordination and decision-making political body is the General Affairs Council (GAC), the monthly meeting of foreign and European affairs ministers, at which I have represented the Commission for five years.

The GAC stands apart compared with other Council formations since it has a specific responsibility for preparing European Council meetings (that is, meetings of our Heads of State or Government). It is a Council that is also special in that it covers the most sensitive areas for the Member States: for instance, the seven-year EU investment budget, known as the multiannual financial framework (MFF). It's actually very telling that this strategic MFF file has been given for negotiation not to the ministers of finance but rather to the Europe ministers. Some (perhaps biased!) sources suggest that it was done this way because ministers of finance instinctively want to cut spending while Europe ministers want to increase it… the same goes for enlargement, for cohesion policies and many other aspects (e.g. economic policy) which have cross-cutting importance and are dealt with directly by the GAC.

My mandate has seen a new, more important, role for the GAC, most notably in preparing the ground for the many EU summits that have been held over the past five years, largely dealing with the economic crisis. As Commission representative in the GAC, I've been able to help prepare and shape the high-level discussions by working closely with ministers and the European Council President, Herman Van Rompuy. The regular presence of the European Council President in the GAC is recognition of the importance of the latter in preparing for and as a follow-up to the European Council conclusions. It isn't very well known but Herman Van Rompuy has frequently used the GAC to test the waters before submitting key strategic orientations or initiatives to the Heads of State and Government and as a way of communicating with national capitals so as to smooth the way in preparing EU summits.

Herman Van Rompuy is known among the members of the European Council for his eternal patience, his steely determination to conclude deals by putting his ego aside and his powers of endurance, with very long summits to chair, without any sleep. He has also cooperated well with Commission President Barroso, holding weekly preparatory meetings. Van Rompuy and I usually sat next to each other in GAC meetings and agreed on our double act or performance since we were pushing for the same priorities. I hope that, in the future, we will be able to pursue this model of good cooperation between the European Council and the Commission for the next term.

To me, this enhanced political role for the monthly meetings of the GAC has clearly paid off, allowing us to reach swift and decisive decisions on a number of vital issues, from tackling the economic crisis to finally agreeing on a long-term EU budget (the multi-annual financial framework) or on actual and potential new EU Member States.

New voting arrangements (the extension of qualified majority voting) introduced by the Lisbon Treaty also mean that Member States generally work harder to find consensus. At the end of the day, even if Council decision-making remains mostly consensual, decisions are made faster thanks to the pressure (or threat) of qualified majority voting. In that context, my frequent contacts with national ministers have enabled me to play a coordination and facilitator role within the wider EU decision-making process.

We can and should do more, nonetheless, to improve Council planning and coordination. I am pleased to see that the latest Council presidencies have taken on board the concept that I have been trying to push forward these past years: intensifying our work on better planning, with a roadmap to prepare decisions by sectorial Councils, and also – this is of great importance – focusing on actually implementing European Council conclusions.

We still do need to reduce the 'implementation gap', between decisions being made and action being taken, for which we are paying a high price in terms of trust from the citizens. We often have a big summit, important decisions are taken and then... *nothing*. Nothing, because it takes us a very long time to implement – if at all – the decisions of the Heads of State and Government. So it should really be up to the GAC to better prepare the work, by distributing the tasks coming from European Council to the different Council formations and by doing better *ex post* checking. Enhanced monitoring is indispensable. That way, we will make sure that the decisions adopted at the highest level are actually implemented on the ground.

## The European Parliament as a fully fledged co-legislator

The Lisbon Treaty has considerably beefed up the role of the European Parliament, making it a fully-fledged co-legislator with the Council.

At the start of my mandate as Commissioner for inter-institutional relations, I needed to find a new way of working with the European Parliament that took into account the new law-making process set out in the Lisbon Treaty. That is why in 2011 I negotiated a new long-term agreement between the European Parliament and the Commission, designed to put flesh on the bones of our 'special partnership'. It strengthened the political responsibility of the Commission and improved the working arrangements and the flow of information between the two institutions.

But this agreement was not just about pushing bits of paper around: it was about establishing a whole new way of communicating with the Parliament, including more regular and intensive political dialogue. In practice, this means ensuring that my fellow Commissioners, senior Commission experts, or myself, are available to discuss policy issues with MEPs on a regular basis, in committees and plenaries.

In preparing the Commission work programme, I have made sure that the European Parliament has been extensively involved. The ways in which this has been done have included:

the introduction of President Barroso's State of the Union address, which triggers a lively debate in plenary on the EU's top priorities; the so-called 'structured dialogue' between Commissioners and the competent parliamentary committees; the crucial input of all their respective chairs in the European Parliament's Conference of Committee Chairs (meeting once a year with the entire College, and having several preparatory meetings with me); bilateral meetings with the presidents of political groups (in the framework of the Conference of Presidents); the presentation of the work programme to the plenary by the President of the Commission or myself – I could carry on… The result is that all Parliament's bodies are now involved in some way or another in discussing with the Commission the preparation and implementation of its work programme.

This pragmatic approach also applies to the adoption of legislation. Long gone are the days where the Parliament was merely *consulted* by the Council. Now co-decision (or the ordinary legislative procedure, as it is now formally known) – the procedure which places the European Parliament and the Council on a strictly equal footing as co-legislators – accounts for around 90% of the files.

It has been my experience that despite rather long – and in some cases even nocturnal – plenary debates, numerous amendments and at times difficult internal coordination in the Parliament (due to the conflicting positions of European political groups and national delegations), overall the European Parliament as a co-legislator has proved of immense added value to democratic decision-making. On our EU seven-year investment budget/priority spending, for instance, it is thanks to the resolute pressure of the European Parliament that we managed to improve the overall results of the negotiations – making sure that we could deliver on our growth and jobs agenda, introduce flexibility in the execution of the budget, secure a revision clause and set up a high-level inter-institutional group on 'own resources' which will suggest possible improvement on the revenue side before the end of 2014. It is also thanks to the European Parliament that we have secured an early frontloading of the youth guarantee scheme, accelerated the setting up of the banking union, and made it easier for scientists and researchers to benefit from EU grants. There are indeed hundreds of such examples where the European Parliament has made a world of difference to EU policy outcomes, to the benefit of citizens.

Within the ordinary legislative procedure, or co-decision procedure, most deals are further made as first reading agreements. This is thanks to good cooperation between the three institutions, notably through the development of trilogues (i.e informal contacts between the co-legislators and the Commission) in order to reach agreement. The number of trilogues is impressive, having gone from 167 in 2010 to more than 500 in 2013. In that framework, we in the Commission work very closely with both the Council presidency and European Parliament rapporteur. We pay equal attention to the working groups of the Council and parliamentary committees. And on the national government side – and I am talking here not only about the Council rotating presidency, I can say that the understanding and capabilities to deal with the European Parliament have also improved tremendously.

## National parliaments: the latest reinforcements to the democratic control team

National parliaments had for a long time been the 'poor relations' in the EU construction, having been deprived of some of their legislative prerogatives to the benefit of national governments negotiating directly in the EU Council.

When I took office I was determined to anchor the national parliaments better to the EU decision-making process. That is why I personally undertook to visit all national parliaments over the course of the past five years, discussing ways for them to play a more proactive part in EU policy making through the 'political dialogue' process launched by President Barroso.

The Commission now sends all its legislative proposals and consultation documents to national parliaments, which may then submit their own opinions on these proposals to the Commission for reply. The idea is to make sure that all new EU proposals are fit-for-purpose at the national level, and to make sure that they are better coordinated with national policy-making procedures and priorities.

This is all part of our effort to dispel the perception that 'Brussels imposes legislation on national governments': in fact, the decision-making process at EU level is extremely inclusive, and many different levels of governance can have their say before proposals pass into law.

It is clear that our efforts to raise awareness of this process among national parliaments have borne fruit. This systematic consultation, combined with the subsidiarity check mechanism, the dynamic exchanges within inter-parliamentary bodies such as COSAC (the bi-annual conference of members of national parliamentary EU committees and representatives of the European Parliament) and the bilateral visits to and hearings of Commissioners by national parliaments, have led to a greater understanding of EU policies and a marked increase in the amount of detailed feedback and suggestions from national parliaments on proposed EU legislation.

As a result, the Commission has received well over 2000 opinions from national parliaments since the political dialogue was launched in 2006, culminating in almost 600 opinions from national parliaments in 2013 alone.

Since the Lisbon Treaty came into force at the end of 2009, national parliaments have also had a new right to question the 'added value' of EU legislative proposals. With our multi-level approach to political governance in Europe, it is clear that some issues are best handled at the local, regional or national rather than EU level, depending on their nature and size. That's why the Lisbon Treaty gave national parliaments as a group the right to object to proposed EU legislation if enough of them consider

*The increasing engagement of national parliaments in dialogue with the Commission.*

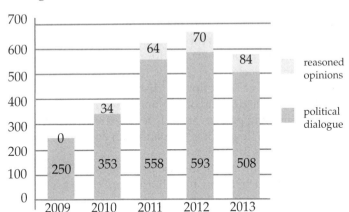

that the matter can best be legislated at a different level, in line with what we call the principle of subsidiarity.

The procedure here is slightly different than the broader political dialogue: if national parliaments disagree with proposals from the Commission setting out an EU-wide approach for a particular policy area, believing instead that a national or even subnational approach is more efficient, then they must set out the specific reasons behind their thinking in their opinion to the Commission.

Since this new power for national parliaments came into force at the start of the present Commission mandate, it too has become increasingly popular, with over 250 reasoned opinions from national parliaments, a clear indication of their increasing desire to play an active and effective role in better EU law-making.

This process also allows national parliaments to show a 'yellow card' to the Commission if enough of them (one third, in most cases) are concerned about a specific proposal. So far, there have been only two such cards – one on proposals that national parliaments were concerned would impinge upon people's right to strike, the other on the creation of a European public prosecutor's office – where a sufficient number of national parliaments believed that national action was more appropriate than European.

The first yellow card led us to withdraw the proposal, because of insufficient political support for it from national parliaments as well as the European Parliament and Member State governments. On the second one, the European public prosecutor's office, we decided to maintain the Commission's proposal after careful examination and concluding that there was indeed a legitimate reason for producing an EU-wide initiative, since protection of the EU budget against fraud can be better achieved at the EU – rather than solely national – level. On several occasions, I explained the Commission position to national parliaments which had issued a negative opinion, highlighting the very low successful investigation rate or recovery of lost assets – caused mainly by cross-border problems like inadmissibility of evidence or lack of cooperation of investigators in cross-border fraud against the EU budget. It was clear that unanimity could not be achieved, but many justice and interior ministers spoke highly of these proposals, thus opening the door to enhanced cooperation, with a third of Member States ready to go that way. I do hope that others will join us subsequently.

This process of subsidiarity checking is in any case not merely about what is right or wrong. It is about how best to tackle very difficult and complex issues which have both national and European dimensions. This is real EU-level democracy at work: making sure that national parliaments have the opportunity to give their opinions and that EU institutions – in particular the Commission – respond to them. Talking with national parliaments, listening to their views and understanding their concerns has undoubtedly helped to shape the decision-making process for the better.

The great added value of the Commission receiving national parliaments' opinions early in the legislative process is that it can conduct negotiations with the European Parliament and the

Council in full awareness of the national parliaments' main concerns and interests.

We must also encourage national parliaments to assume their democratic responsibility in a number of other ways too. For instance, by taking part in the many public consultations that are now standard practice before any new EU legislative proposals are tabled, or by stepping up their discussions with each other and with the European Parliament, to make sure that they coordinate their positions.

I have also put forward another way of reconnecting Europe with its citizens: creating a genuine European legal statute for European political parties. Until now, the European political parties to which national parties usually belong have had to register as NGOs in one EU Member State alone, usually Belgium where the bulk of the European Parliament's political activity is located, and this has prevented them from working efficiently.

As a result, when citizens vote in the European Parliament elections every five years, there is little or no debate about European issues: citizens vote for national parties and often do so based on national issues. Changing the rules on European political parties will allow them to operate across all 28 Member States, bringing an additional European dimension to the political debate and ensuring that European Parliament elections in future more closely reflect Europe-wide rather than purely national issues.

I am therefore happy that towards the end of my mandate as Commissioner for inter-institutional relations and administration we managed to reach an agreement with the Council and the Parliament on this important file.

## Enhanced participatory democracy and transparency

Here we are talking about an issue which is particularly close to my heart: citizens' direct involvement in the shaping of policies.

My ambition as Commissioner has been to lay down the foundations of the first ever instrument of *transnational partici-*

*patory democracy* – the European Citizens' Initiative (ECI), a necessary supplement to (but, I should add, by no means a substitute for) *representative democracy*.

Since the instrument is brand new, it may merit a brief presentation.

Launched in April 2012, the ECI allows citizens from across the EU to focus policy-makers' attention on the things that really matter to them. Broadly speaking, any idea that wins support from more than one million people across the EU has to be considered by the Commission and could eventually form the basis of formal proposals for new legislation across all 28 Member States.

At the time of writing, over 5 million citizens have already signed up to 24 different initiatives on issues ranging from cross-border mobility and pan-European voting rights to roaming charges, media pluralism and environmental management.

Two initiatives have already reached the one-million signature mark. The first is on the management of water, the second is on embryo research. A third – against animal testing – has also reached one million but is still being formally submitted to the Commission. The first two initiatives have had public hearings organised in the European Parliament. The first one – the 'right to water' – has been formally considered by the Commission and I am glad that we said yes, with a substantial list of commitments for the coming months and years. As a result of this first ever exercise of pan-European citizen-driven democracy, there will be improvements in water quality, infrastructure and sanitation that will benefit people both in Europe and in developing countries.

All this is promising. And it's only the beginning. Some of the future initiatives will undoubtedly make it onto the EU statute books. And they all generate a pan-European debate between citizens, what Jürgen Habermas refers to as the formation of a European public sphere – with citizens from all walks of life able to discuss and make their voices heard directly in shaping policy-making at EU level. The ECI by its very nature addresses issues that affect people across the EU and brings together citizens from all walks of life and from all four corners of Europe. It provides a unique opportunity for a truly pan-European debate between citizens, about what matters to them.

I have had the opportunity to meet with organisers of such initiatives. I have seen their commitment. We've gone to great lengths in the Commission to help them overcome the initial technical difficulties, most notably by making our own servers available for their online collection and providing technical assistance. I have also discussed at length with Member States how to make sure that they could comply with their part of the deal, in particular as far as the verification of the online collection system and validation of signatures are concerned. All actors have had to adapt to this new transnational instrument: the organisers, the Commission, the European Parliament, the Member States.

We're at an early stage. But it's a first important step in developing EU transnational e-democracy. Some experts even see the possibility of pan-European 'electronic referendums' taking place in the not-too-distant future.

When I present the importance of ECI to Member States I try to show them a picture that goes beyond what we have now. I point out that in a few years we could all have e-ID cards, which would allow us, citizens, not only to hold our health records and personal data on the chips but also to participate in democratic e-debate more thoroughly. Citizens will be increasingly involved in EU public affairs through e-government. Estonia is pioneering this endeavour.

The digital revolution starts in the classroom. Education materials are changing, together with the business models of our universities. And so is the way in which public authorities and government provide services and interact with citizens. The internet constitutes a formidable window of opportunity. It enables us to engage with the younger generation through social media (Facebook, twitter, EUtube, google+ etc.), with short targeted messages and exchanges. If used correctly it should enable policy-makers to alert youngsters, to debate with them and provide them with some of the keys to understanding what is taking place in Europe and the world.

I believe the development of e-signatures and social networks thus has great potential to foster participatory democracy and to contribute to the development of a European public sphere, involving citizens more directly in the shaping of political action. Politicians need to engage actively, for the failure to establish easily accessible communication channels is what ultimately risks paving the ways to more populism and extremism across the continent.

We saw with ACTA (the anti-counterfeiting trade agreement which aimed to help countries work together to tackle large-scale intellectual property rights violations more effectively) that the power of social media cannot be understated. The communication deficit on the part of the Commission constituted an open avenue for protestors to spread only the negative impacts of ACTA. In a very short period of time people got from their computer screens to the streets (in Germany, Poland and the Netherlands) and in no time the European Parliament had received a petition signed by almost 2.5 million people calling on it to refuse to ratify the agreement. ACTA was rejected by the European Parliament in July 2012. Governments backed off. Debate was impossible. This to me was a case in point of too slow, too little, too late in e-engaging with the citizens.

*Enhanced transparency*

Finally, reconnecting with citizens is not just about making sure that the EU is seen as being democratically legitimate and accountable – it is also about making sure that it is transparent and fair.

Despite a widespread perception to the contrary, the Commission is traditionally a very transparent administration. However this is little known. To counter this, I have set up the 'transparency internet portal' to offer a one-stop shop on all details concerning the way decisions are prepared, who participates in preparing them, and what documents are produced as part or as a result of this process. Citizens are thus offered a single point of access to all recent public consultations, the impact assessments made, the expert groups or other entities consulted, the register of Commission documents, the Commissioners' declarations of interests, the ethics rules concerning civil servants, information on the recipients of EU funds, etc.

Since we are talking about consultation: the Commission has a duty to listen to all sides of the policy argument – an obligation to consult widely with all interested parties on policy proposals is written into the Treaties – but managing this process properly is vital to make sure that lobbyists and interest groups do not have undue influence.

Lobbying often carries a negative connotation. In the EU 'continental' mind (i.e. less so with our British friends), it is often associated with somebody – a consultant – secretly, and therefore suspiciously, pushing for a business-oriented interest. It need not be that way. Lobbying should not be a secret matter. It must be done in the daylight. And it does not only involve business: its scope is much wider. I can tell you that some of the NGOs in the environment, consumer protection or human rights fields are particularly forceful and convincing campaigners or advocacy groups! Therefore we chose to embrace the wider concept that, to participate in and shape the EU agenda, all civil society organisations – whatever the interest they represent – should do it in an open and transparent way.

That's why I've worked closely with the European Parliament to develop the most ambitious joint transparency register in the world, in terms of its scope and significance. Launched in 2011, today this register contains data on over 30,000 individuals working for around 75% of the professional lobby firms operating in Brussels, around 60% of the NGOs and many other civil society organisations, from faith groups and think tanks to law firms and regional authorities, who try in some way to influence EU policy and decision-making. All in all, more than

6,500 organisations are registered (May 2014 data), including the likes of British Telecommunications (BT), Gazprom, Amcham, European Trade Union Confederation (ETUC), Greenpeace, Human Rights Watch, Burson Marsteller.... And while registration is voluntary, it is clear from the continuing rise in the number of registrations that most of the individuals or organisations wishing to consult with the Commission or Parliament understand that they need to register in advance. This is the only way that both Commission staff and civil society organisations alike can be certain that their discussions are open and honest, and that no undue influence is being asserted.

*Transparency Register - total number of registrations*

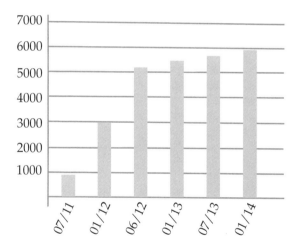

# 3.  A MULTISPEED EUROPE?

Well, yes, a multispeed Europe is already here. The Eurozone has eighteen EU countries inside; eight are still to join; two have opted out. There are abstentions from the Schengen open borders (UK, Ireland and Cyprus; Bulgaria, Romania and Croatia to join later) and the Area of Freedom and Security (UK, Ireland and Denmark). Enhanced cooperation in specific areas (e.g. on divorce law or the EU patent) is being developed.

And this process will intensify. It is unrealistic to expect 28 countries (or more in the future) to be able and/or to want to move forward on all policies at the same speed. The tendency will be accelerated by the development of the Eurozone.

## The Eurozone as a core gravitational force (the centre)

*To help understand our EU galaxy, I'd like to use a 'solar system' metaphor:*

Members States can be seen as planets of differing size and features, with the Eurozone making a core.

The Eurozone has created a gravitational force where the relationships among its Member States will be increasingly governed by various legal and political commitments. The fiscal compact goes to show that the Eurozone will do whatever it takes to preserve the EU currency.

The basis for participation in the system is adherence not only to the EU core policies – most notably the single market and its accompanying policies – but also the sharing of a single currency (for Eurozone members).

## Orbits and distances from the centre

The Member States orbit around the Eurozone core at different speeds and distances. Member States that are closer to the core travel more quickly because they are more affected by the Eurozone's gravitational attraction. The distance and speed also depends on each planet's characteristics. Some Member States move slowly, in distant orbits, though part of the same planetary system.

The UK and Denmark, for example, have opt-outs from the euro. The UK makes sure that it keeps its distance from the Eurozone. Meanwhile all other EU countries are or can potentially become part of the Eurozone. Each country will do so at its own speed.

But distance from the centre does not mean that a given Member State is not interested in the gravitational force developing. *Even opt-out countries have a direct interest in seeing more integration elsewhere in the EU.* As British Prime Minister David Cameron has reiterated on various occasions, the UK has an interest in the Eurozone succeeding. I quote from one of his speeches to UK business leaders (on 17 May 2012):

> The Eurozone is at crossroads. It either has to make-up or it is looking at a potential break-up... Either Europe has a committed, stable, successful Eurozone with an effective firewall, well capitalised and regulated banks, a system of fiscal burden sharing,

and supportive monetary policy across the Eurozone. Or we are in uncharted territory, which carries huge risks for everybody.

Of course such differentiated integration needs to remain an open process to make sure that the common interest always prevails over the individual interest of each of its members. Inclusion rather than exclusion is therefore the rule of thumb. This also applies to countries outside the EU with actual (officially: Iceland, Montenegro, the former Yugoslav Republic of Macedonia, Serbia and Turkey) or potential (officially: Albania, Bosnia and Herzegovina and Kosovo) candidate status.

In the same vein, there should be no institutional segregation inside the EU. Institutions need to be common to all EU countries (inside and outside the Eurozone) and pathways need to exist between the centre and the periphery. Concretely speaking, the European Commission continues to fulfil its role of initiation and surveillance for both the Eurozone and wider EU, and the Eurozone summits are chaired by the European Council President and enlarged to all EU States whenever possible.

## The EU 'galaxy'

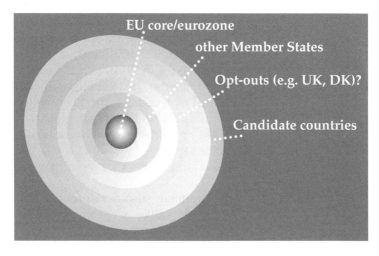

## The United Kingdom

Where does the UK stand in this system? We hear a lot about it 'sleepwalking to the EU exit door'.

Let me be clear. *That would be a colossal failure for both the EU and the UK.* It would be economically devastating for the latter. And it would diminish the political weight of the former.

We are simply too interdependent. We need each other. And therefore, we must find all possible ways to preserve our relationship.

It will not be easy. There is a genuine communication issue in the UK. Most of the media and many political leaders take any opportunity to blame the EU – resorting to 'EU-bashing' and caricature. The media misinformation is, unfortunately, not rebutted by official-level communication, which carries on criticising the EU, despite the efforts of the Commission's Representation to put the record straight in terms of facts sent to journalists. The Commission Representation's website in the UK has a long 'euromyths' section, rebutting press 'scoops' by tabloids which often attack the EU for things it has not actually done. If we were to believe such newspapers as the *Sun*, the *Daily Mail*, the *Daily Express* or the *Daily Telegraph*, the EU must take the blame for decisions taken by the European Court of Human rights – which is not even an EU institution but a Council of Europe one (founded by the UK in 1948). To believe these newspapers, the EU would force the UK to abolish national birth and death certificates and replace them with EU-branded ones; the EU would force producers to ban 'made in Britain' tags from high quality British products; it would force households to use five different bins to recycle rubbish… I could continue the long list of EU-bashing myths that are all simply untrue!

So, it's not easy to change the innate suspicions promoted for years by media and political leaders alike, or to convey the idea that the UK's destiny can only be in Europe. But we have to do it. We need to try to get the message across through all the available channels – pro-European political leaders, the Confederation of British Industry (CBI), think tanks, parliamentarians, trade unions, etc. The UK has a very strong democratic tradition which, despite some people's tactical and populist agendas, can and should be used to show the mutual benefits of UK membership (for both the UK and the EU).

These benefits have been measured. The UK represents around 12% of the EU's population and 15% of its economy; the EU accounts for close to 50% of UK exports, and the UK contributes up to €6.5 billion of the EU budget (net). As a key Member State the UK has contributed extensively to the single market, EU trade and economic policy, the enlargement process, and the anchoring of many of the Member States to the transatlantic alliance. The UK possesses one of the EU's strongest industrial bases, has important diplomatic and military resources and has long served as a bridge between the EU and the US. English is the EU's lingua franca... I could carry on.

The Confederation of British Industry estimates that EU membership is worth the equivalent of £3,000 per year for each and every UK household. It is also very clearly opposed to the UK leaving the EU, for pragmatic reasons: half the UK's total trade is with the EU, and when it comes to negotiating with other trading partners outside Europe, the EU carries the clout of a market of 500 million consumers (as opposed to the UK's 60 million). London's role as the EU's main financial centre would be endangered. The UK would also cease to participate in the EU's decision-making process: if it left the EU, market access by the UK (e.g. signing of a free trade agreement) is unlikely to come without obligations on the regulatory side, including the adoption of EU rules – but, this time, without any ability to influence them from the inside.

As Polish Foreign Minister Radek Sikorski has argued regarding the scenario of the UK striking a deal with the EU after it had left – and I quote:

British Eurosceptics… say the British government could negotiate a trade deal that preserved all the advantages of membership in the single market without any of the political and financial costs. My answer to that: don't count on it. Many European states would hold a grudge against a country which, in their view, had selfishly left the EU (21 September 2012 speech at Oxford).

The City of London, too, has warned about the hugely negative impact of a possible UK exit from the EU, highlighting the many advantages of the single market for the British economy.

In the UK, these arguments need to be heard beyond the closed circles of high-level political, economic and financial experts.

And *at EU level, we ought to take the UK's request for reforms seriously*. As ever – the on-going debate in the UK provides a window of opportunity to address the challenges of reform. How can we reform our economic governance without undermining the integrity of the single market? How do we establish the foundations for smart and sustainable growth in the EU? How do we address the social consequences of the crisis? How do we further reduce red tape? How do we reinforce democratic accountability and the ownership of decisions taken at EU level? How can EU citizens reclaim their grip on the EU project? These are big questions, which we can only tackle together.

# 4. OUT OF THE CRISIS, STRONGER?

The crisis took us by surprise – there can be no doubt about that. *It hit us like a storm in the middle of the ocean*: we had left the shores of *monetary* union – having adopted the single currency and created an independent European Central Bank – but without having reached the other side, that of *fiscal and economic* union. While we were navigating visually, in the open sea, the winds started to blow strongly against us: our weakest members were on the point of falling overboard, and our whole ship was even at risk of capsizing; we had to battle as hard as we could, with everyone on deck, baling out water, making use of every bucket we could find until finally – and only just – we managed to reach calmer waters, thanks to the whole crew's effort and determination. But the storm left its mark… it made us realise we were simply ill equipped to withstand such a financial crisis. We had no option but to accelerate the move towards the shores of financial and economic integration…

## Why has the crisis been so severe? Why did it take us so long to adjust?

Populist parties and EU detractors are quick to blame the euro for the creation of the crisis that we have been through. I think that on this we ought to set the record straight.

First, the financial storm was generated not in the EU but on the other side of the Atlantic, with the US subprime bubble and the collapse of Lehman Brothers, which was as you may recall one of the largest private investment banks in the world. This led to the draining of interbank lending – in the context of an already pretty depressed US economy – and the bursting of the financial bubble on a world scale.

Second, the crisis hit some EU Member States particularly hard as they had accumulated excessively high levels of both private and public debt, on which they had built their – until then – rather artificial growth. Structural reforms had been postponed as a result, leading to a loss of competitiveness and macroeconomic imbalances. These domestic accumulated debts were nothing short of a time-bomb. Sooner or later it would have exploded.

There were a lot of negative factors at national level that piled on top of each other:

– Irresponsible budgeting (e.g. in Greece where fiscal weakness was clearly the cause of the crisis);
– A toxic interconnection between sovereign debts and the banking sector (the latter holding significant amounts of the former);
– Economic and financial – linked to a housing – bubbles;
– Imbalances caused by loss of competitiveness and lack of skills in the workforce to cope with changes in the economy.

This all led to a collapse of financial markets, notably in Greece, Portugal, Spain and Ireland with a domino effect on other countries – putting at risk the whole of the EU, and destabilising the world economy. This resulted in turn in a loss of confidence among private investors and the financial markets in the ability of some governments to repay their debts (which translated into the wide spread between e.g. Greek and German bonds).

Ultimately our collective inability to act was very severely judged by our citizens. I say 'collective' inability for I do not only mean that of the policy-makers. The loss of trust was first directed against the financial services industry and at certain speculators whose behaviour clearly contributed to damaging the real economy. Likewise, at some CEOs of big multinational companies who were – indeed some still are – making profits in one country while employing sophisticated accounting devices to make sure they pay only minimal taxes on those profits in tax havens.

At the end of the day taxpayers found themselves having to pay for the misconduct of others, and this produced an acute and understandable sense of injustice. The worsening of the public finances meant that we had to continue borrowing and paying debt interest instead of being able to invest in the real economy (infrastructure, education, research and innovation etc.), to the benefit of our citizens. Of course we – politicians – also bear a direct responsibility for letting this happen, in the slow and originally uncoordinated response to the crisis. This has no doubt accounted for the decline in public trust vis-à-vis national institutions and the EU as a whole, now at record-low levels since the bursting of the financial bubble. A large number of EU prime ministers have lost office since the start of the crisis, voted out by their electorates. Electoral volatility has been exacerbated by the crisis, with high levels of voter abstention, a movement away from the mainstream political parties and a strengthening of the most extreme populist parties.

*A glimpse of hope, however*: according to the Eurobarometer opinion polls a majority of EU citizens continue to support economic and monetary union with a single currency, despite the turmoil! Our fellow citizens seem to consider that the euro is not the problem, but rather part of the solution and certainly an important bond that we must strive to preserve… and in that they are certainly right!

It is true to say that many countries' problems – the time-bomb of profligate public spending, rigid labour markets, and competitiveness gaps – date back to long before the euro was even launched. And it is also true that the euro – still a very young currency – has managed to remain a very strong  currency (some would even say *too strong*). It has remained a safe haven currency, of global use, that allows us to exchange transparently and freely in the Eurozone and inspires trust.

Rather than creating difficulties for us, our single currency has helped us tremendously through the crisis.

## So what lessons did we learn?

We had a monetary union but we acted as if monetary interdependence was sustainable without further economic integration and a genuine European budget. We overlooked the fact that the integration of economies and financial markets had outpaced these developments; it was simply not on the radar screen of the EU.

We found ourselves with a common – even a single – monetary policy but without having reached the same level of fiscal and economic integration. In a shock situation, a single market with a single currency but without a commensurate common budget or genuine borrowing capacity had exacerbated the divergences between countries.

On top of this, it took us a while to realise that individual Member States could not deal with this crisis on their own or coordinate their responses with each other, i.e. that the inter-governmental method alone was clearly unable to cope.

To come back to the consequences of monetary policy: I think that we had underestimated what the euro implied, both symbolically and objectively. The sharing of a currency is one of the most intimate bonds – *it requires a totally new system for sharing sovereignty*. It becomes necessary to look at each others' budgets and how they are financed, at social and employment policy, at education, pensions, and so on.

Still, we did realise that we needed new tools, requiring a complete revamp of economic governance. What we faced was living proof that to fight the global crisis it was not *less* but rather *more* Europe that was needed: strengthened budgetary and economic coordination, a much better regulated banking sector and more independent banking supervision to allow de-coupling of bank risks and sovereign debts. The euro helped us avoid losing some defaulting countries that would have had to resort to competitive devaluations, and suffered uncontrolled inflation and debt strangulation. It forced a collective response to avoid more collateral damage. And it propelled a move towards more integration.

As a result, an impressive range of measures were adopted to make sure we could keep our heads above water: rescue mechanisms, reinforced budgetary and economic surveillance, banking supervision…

## How does this new economic and financial governance work? What instruments did we put in place?

### *Rescue mechanisms and financial firewalls*

I will never forget the College where perhaps for the first time in history we had a session on a Sunday. It was because of the situation in Greece – which was on the verge of financial collapse. It was 9 May 2010. We were probably literally hours away from the so-called 'Grexit', which could have forced Greece out of the Eurozone, and possibly out of the EU.

We felt an immense sense of responsibility… history looking at us. It was one of these defining moments: *saving Europe or starting the process of a bitter unravelling of all the European integration put together over the past sixty years.*

After hours of discussions, we managed to agree on a system of economic rescue which I must say was very similar to the one that is in place right now. But at the time it was not supported by the EU finance ministers, who decided instead to go for an intergovernmental approach and a very complicated system of bilateral assistance. Yes, in the end this did save the day, but we paid a high price for this approach – the costs got bigger, the crisis longer, and the consequences in the form of loss of trust in the EU and national decision makers just grew.

This is what is sometime so frustrating about the EU. We already pretty much knew the 'contours', the shape of the final decision but we needed to go through this process of 'political fermentation' – through a process of letting this decision mature – to accept that in the globalised economy, under the pressure of such a severe crisis, only collective decision-making can save an individual Member State. As President Barroso had put it 'we would either swim together or sink separately'.

We had thus devised a Europe-wide solidarity mechanism right from the start – it just took the Council a bit more time to realise that this, rather than bilateral aids, was the right path.

As a result, in May 2010 the EU put in place a rescue package of more than €100 billion, but this was solely in the form of bilateral loans. It then set up two temporary mechanisms: the European Financial Stability Facility (EFSF) and the European Financial Stabilisation Mechanism (EFSM) with a total lending capacity of €500 billion. These instruments were the first expression of our Member States' financial solidarity.

As these two backstops were set up as temporary funds, the euro area countries in the autumn of 2012 created a new and permanent financial backstop: the European Stability Mechanism (ESM), with a lending capacity set at €500 billion. Financial assistance will be available to those countries who have ratified the treaty on stability, coordination and governance (also known as the 'fiscal compact') on condition that macroeconomic adjustment programmes are implemented. In exchange for the implementation of adjustment programmes, some countries are thus given access to the ESM to remedy the difficulties they experienced in repaying their debts. This permanent 'firewall' aims to prevent contagion in the Eurozone and to restore confidence in financial markets .

The European Central Bank (ECB) also played a major part in restoring market confidence. Its president, Mario Draghi, promised in particular that his institution 'would do whatever it takes' to save the euro. In August 2012 the ECB – which according to its charter is prohibited from purchasing government bonds directly from their issuers – announced the possibility of purchasing sovereign debt on the secondary market. This readiness to stretch its mandate to the limit helped restore market confidence. It also enabled the refinancing of countries with difficulties and exercised downward pressure on the interest rates to be repaid, without a single euro spent by the European taxpayer. Hats off to the ECB and its president for their response!

As shown by both the ESM and the ECB interventions, one of the premises of EU action is that solidarity and responsibility should always go hand in hand. The EU's objective is to combine more solidarity and financial support with more responsibility, in the form of fiscal consolidation and structural reforms aimed at fostering competitiveness and labour market reform. Progress on both budgetary solidarity and structural reform has already been quite remarkable.

To pursue reforms further what we need at EU level is to develop *a genuine fiscal capacity*, beyond the ceilings of the multiannual financial framework, our seven-year investment budget. We need to offer incentives and support – in the form of bilateral 'contractual arrangements', or 'convergence partnerships' as the European Parliament proposes to call them – for the Member States to be able to undertake the necessary important national economic, social and active labour market policy reforms in the current context of budgetary constraint.

These partnerships would involve some kind of voluntary compliance on the part of both the EU and the Member States. And this genuine fiscal capacity could rely on *a system of genuine own resources*, which is currently being examined by the EU institutions under the leadership of Mario Monti. I am participating directly in this inter-institutional group and I trust that Mario Monti's exemplary experience and credibility will deliver very positive results.

In terms of financing, we also need to dig deeper into the possibility of issuing eurobonds to borrow directly from the markets and reduce financial fragmentation. To manage the revenue (and borrowing) side of the EU budget, an EU treasury would ultimately need to be created inside the Commission and this portfolio could be given to a Commission Vice-President.

All in all, we can see that the solidarity and responsibility mechanisms that have been put in place are calling for more, rather than less, financial integration in the EU.

## Banking union with a single supervisor and a single resolution mechanism

Here our main objectives have been to decouple bank risks from sovereign debts and to make sure that the banking sector is much more prudently governed. We owe this to our taxpayers.

It is no mean task. It involves a swathe of regulations to strengthen bank capitalisation, governance and supervision.

Thanks to the relentless work of my colleague Michel Barnier, an impressive regulatory framework has been achieved. I will give you a few examples:

– Prudential rules have been beefed up for banks to provide some guarantee in terms of minimum capital and liquidity requirements;

- The European Systemic Risk Board in Frankfurt has been set up and is responsible for the macro-prudential oversight of the banking industry;
- Three new pan-European financial supervisory authorities have been established (the European Banking Authority in London, the European Insurance and Occupational Pensions Authority in Frankfurt and the European Securities and Markets Authority in Paris);
- A new independent single supervisory mechanism (given to the ECB) will replace the national regulators for banks in the Eurozone and in any other Member State wishing to participate, and will implement the single rulebook developed for all banks operating in the single market;
- Savers' money is guaranteed (up to €100,000 per depositor per bank) to avoid massive withdrawals in case of bank failure;
- Last, but not least: a single resolution mechanism has also been adopted to make sure that banks – as opposed to taxpayers – pay for their failures.

As a result our banking sector is better governed, supervised and capitalised. This is most impressive if we look at where we were five years ago. Unprecedented, even.

## Fiscal and economic union

My other colleague, Olli Rehn, has been instrumental in setting in motion a collective strategy to assess and have Member States coordinate their budgetary and economic plans throughout the year. To this end, the powers of the Commission and the Council to monitor national budgets and economic policies have been substantially reinforced. As I said before, to monitor does not mean to decide instead of a Member State! It means being given the possibility of discussing fiscal and economic policies before their adoption and implementation by national authorities.

Our tool for this is known as the 'European semester' (which was set up in 2011). This is the EU integrated planning, coordinating and reporting system steered by the Commission. This European semester integrates the technical instruments that we hear about in the press: the 'six-pack', 'two-pack', 'stability and growth pact', 'fiscal compact', etc.

Through the European semester we have substantially strengthened fiscal and economic policy coordination and surveillance at EU level. In a nutshell: the Commission sets out priorities (in its November annual growth survey) to guide Member States when designing their budget and economic reform plans for the next year, screening any imbalances that need correction. On this basis, Member States submit their budget and economic reform plans in April and the Commission issues tailored policy advice in its proposed 'country specific recommendations' immediately after that.

As a result the Member States and the Commission discuss among themselves – in the European Council but also in the different Council formations – topics like the reforms in France, the German trade surplus, the financial sector in Spain, specific problems in Greece etc. Decisions are taken by the summer of each year by the Council on the basis of Commission recommendations. Unless they are opposed (by qualified majority in the Council), corrective measures – even sanctions – can be adopted upon a proposal from the Commission if a country does not take sufficient action to comply with budget rules (the excessive deficit procedure) or does not propose an adequate plan of action to correct excessive macroeconomic imbalances. In this way, we avoid what happened in 2003 where the European Council undermined the stability and growth pact by turning a blind eye to the breaches made by Germany and France.

Eurozone budgetary surveillance now intensifies towards the end of the year with the Commission submitting its opinion on each Eurozone country's draft budget plan. The Commission can raise the alarm if it sees that a national budget is going in the wrong direction. It is then discussed with the other Member

States. This national semester (assessment of national draft budgets) goes to show that EU surveillance is entering into areas that are in the hard-core of national sovereignty.

*This surveillance cycle and related Member State commitments were virtually unthinkable a few years ago.*

The EU is now much better equipped to face a future storm of similar magnitude. Thanks – it has to be said – to the financial crisis of 2008, the EU has supplemented its monetary union by the foundations of an economic, fiscal and banking union. But to prevent future crises we also need to move decisively from an originally *reactive* to a *proactive* and longer-term approach.

## Are we on a sustainable growth path?

Can we now be sure we are on a path of sustainable growth? Unfortunately, no – not as yet.

As a result of this new collective governance architecture, the euro-area economy is slowly moving out of recession, after five years of downturn. Data from the second and third quarters of 2013 showed a gradual recovery (of respectively +0.3% and +0.2%). GDP is now expected to grow by 1.2% in 2014 in the euro area (and 1.6% in the whole of the EU) and by 1.7% in 2015 (2% in the EU). Budget deficits have been more than halved and are projected to decline to 2.6% of GDP in the EU and 2.5% of GDP in the euro area. We have also seen investor and consumer confidence coming back, and financial markets stabilising.

Ireland and Portugal have successfully ended their bail-out programmes and Spain has exited the specific programme it had for its banks. Business confidence and moderate growth seem to be back. All have returned to the financial markets, so to speak, and it is in these three (full or partial) programme countries that productivity has also most improved since 2010. Greece's painful efforts are, finally, starting to bear fruit with a primary budget surplus in 2014, a return to the bond markets and even slight growth forecast for 2014. Cyprus, where adjustment started later, could see a turnaround in 2015. Latvia, which had suffered a severe crisis, has managed to turn its economy around with the help of the EU/IMF led programmes and is now one of the – if not *the* – fastest growing economies in the EU and the Eurozone´s latest newcomer.

But this is no time for rejoicing.

First, the levels of growth remain modest. Whether they will be sustained remains to be seen. And the employment and social consequences of the crisis are still very much being felt by our fellow citizens. Unemployment is high, at 12% for the EU as a whole and with large disparities across Member States (rates are more than 25% in Greece and Spain). This represents more than 26 million men and women who are currently unemployed in the EU – almost 10 million more than five years ago.

The crisis has hit young people particularly hard. Youth unemployment is currently at almost 25% (more than 50% in Greece and Spain). An increasing number of people – around 116 million – are living below the poverty line or at risk of poverty or social exclusion. This accounts for nearly 23% of the total EU population. Public debt – although decreasing in some countries – is still at very high levels and constitutes a heavy burden on our youngsters and on future generations. As I said before, repayments on these debts are lost potential investment in infrastructure projects, research and innovation, our education and health systems, etc. And in southern Europe in particular, SMEs continue to find it particularly difficult to access credit and thus investment on affordable terms.

Second, the public perception of how decisions are taken and implemented has been fundamentally damaged. The 'troika' (made up of the Commission, the IMF and the ECB) – 'the men in black', as some journalists like to call them – is vilified by suffering populations. In the public mind, they epitomise the reign of technocracy, with decisions taken by emotionless technocrats coming from respectively Brussels, Washington and Frankfurt, with their black suits and sunglasses, to dictate and unilaterally impose austerity measures on already impoverished populations and help-less governments. 'Brussels', 'the troika', 'the Commission' are amalgamated into one by populist parties and some of the media to summon up the spectre of rule by unelected bureaucrats.

So we need to work on both the social and economic front and also the perception of a lack of democratic accountability.

## The social dimension: the need to work closely with Member States and other key stakeholders

The problems of unemployment and poor social conditions to-gether present one of the biggest, if not *the* biggest, challenges ahead of us.

This is the area where people are struggling most and where the promises of Europe seem to have vanished or to have been broken. If we do not forcefully address these problems we risk losing an entire EU generation that paradoxically has the high-est level of qualifications ever.

First things first: it's worth recording that, under the EU Treaties, social and employment policies are very much the remit of national governments, and indeed there is no particular willingness on their part to transfer these competences to the EU level. Does that mean that nothing can be done at EU level? Certainly not. In the real political world, we should first and foremost look for a pragmatic approach aimed at developing the social dimension of the economic and monetary union.

This can take several forms.

We must encourage the creation of quality jobs: a strong com-mitment from the Member States to implement the Youth Guar-antee is needed in order to ensure that young people receive a decent offer of employment, further education or training within four months of becoming unemployed or leaving formal educa-tion. This could be integrated into a minimum social framework to be offered by the EU, its Member States and all relevant stake-holders (companies, trade unions, etc.) to the younger generations, with support from the European Social Fund and reference to such measures as the Alliance for Apprenticeships.

In addition, the employment and social impacts of our policies need to be very seriously considered. By this I mean several things:

First, for each and every legislative proposal we make we should always ask ourselves: what will be the impact on employment? What will be the social consequences of this proposal? Will it help? Will it make the situation worse? Will it ease the burden on the Member States?

Second, we should continue to strengthen our social and employment coordination and surveillance system. To fight the *debt crisis* we now use the reinforced binding thresholds that we have for our fiscal discipline in general and budget deficits in particular. To fight the *social crisis*, should we not introduce similar kinds of thresholds and take action if, for example, the rate of unemployment or poverty reaches an unacceptable level?

Do we not need to go one step further in the social surveillance of and cooperation with and among Member States? This would enable us to make sure that social imbalances become an integral part of the EU macroeconomic coordination and surveillance mechanism (the European semester). We should make consolidation efforts compatible with employment and poverty reduction targets, so that in case of imbalances, the Commission would trigger the same corrective procedure as for excessive budgetary deficits, potentially resulting in a fine. The social scoreboard of 2014 is a start, to keep better track of Member States' progress in implementing their national job plans. We need to look very seriously at these key employment and social indicators, including those on unemployment, young people who are not in education, employment or training, the real gross disposable income of households, the at-risk-of-poverty rate of the working age population and inequalities – *but with a mechanism that would mirror fiscal surveillance*. Social indicators should be utilised as a triggering mechanism for this reinforced imbalances procedure. Within the EU semester, we resolutely need to find the right balance between fiscal consolidation on the one side, and social/employment objectives and growth-enhancing measures on the other.

Third, additional support should be given in exchange for fulfilling social performance criteria. With this in mind, structural reforms must be pursued through bilateral 'convergence partnerships' between the EU and the Member States. These partnerships come with financial support to incentivise structural changes needed at the national level, notably to implement a genuine social investment strategy and active labour market reform. For 2014-2020, the European Social Fund already earmarks €80 billion, i.e. more than €10 billion per year has been allocated for jobs, training, entrepreneurship and social inclusion; the Youth Employment Initiative has earmarked at least €6 billion over two years to help national authorities combat youth unemployment. More needs to be done. In this area more than any other we need to make the case for a strong link between EU financial commitments and solidarity on the one hand and national ownership and responsibility on the other.

Without sufficient financial resources, all this could be viewed as a straitjacket for painful reforms. Support is needed – through an EU autonomous fiscal capacity – to help finance the necessary active labour policies and social reforms in order to recover employment levels, maintain social protection standards, and reduce poverty. Some measures need to be prioritised: e.g. increasing the resilience of labour markets by improving the effectiveness of employment services and other support measures to help the unemployed find jobs and develop their skills; investing in training and education; facilitating labour mobility; boosting job creation in fast growing sectors such as the green economy, health, and information and communications technology (ICT); finding the right balance between job flexibility and security; reconciling work and private life; social inclusion actions and entrepreneurship support.

In regard to national ownership, these reforms need to be discussed and agreed with EU institutions and at national level by governments – but also with the involvement of national parliaments, social partners, employers' organisations and other civil society actors, so as to ensure joint ownership and effective implementation in the field of employment and social inclusion. We must reinforce social dialogue, involving the social partners extensively in shaping, adopting and implementing EU growth and employment strategies.

Reducing barriers to labour mobility remains a priority. How can we have 26 million people unemployed and high rates of youth unemployment but at the same time 2 million vacancies in ICT? We need to liberate the labour market from bureaucratic hurdles by facilitating cross-border mobility. We need to put more emphasis on training. There needs to be easier recognition of professional qualifications, social security coordination and transparency tools for skills and qualifications. Labour market information systems must help anticipate future skills needs and what posts will need to be filled. EU-wide support structures such as the network of European employment services, Eures, need to provide assistance in recruitment and placement of workers beyond national borders thus creating a truly European labour market.

## The democratic dimension: putting the record straight (on the troika) and reinforcing democratic accountability

Before addressing the issue of democratic accountability, I need to put the record straight on the troika.

The troika is the target of almost every possible criticism, as relayed by the media and some national governments alike. The truth of the matter is that, on the EU side, all decisions taken by the troika are first discussed and agreed upon by all the finance ministers. In the framework of these discussions, every minister has the chance to present his or her views.

The problem is how this is then communicated to the press

by the exact same ministers. I often use the example of the 'lift transformation' which takes place between the Council meeting on the 8th floor of the Justus Lipsius – the Council building – and the 1st floor where each minister meets with their domestic press. It is as though, on this vertical journey (of a couple of minutes – no more), some ministers almost entirely forget what it is they have just discussed and most often have voted for unanimously. When they reach the 1st floor it seems they no longer feel responsible for the tough decisions taken on the 8th; some of them have become past masters at virtually creating the impression that they were not even in the room where the decisions were taken! Hence the lasting impression of citizens that the infamous 'men in black' are the ones – and the only ones – imposing tough measures on the people of Europe, with no prior political endorsement by their countries' representatives.

So, I need to put the facts straight: *this is not the case*. And, if you ask me, we would do much better service to the citizens of Europe if ministers were to courageously admit what it is they voted for and also explain why, in the current context, they needed to take some difficult decisions, to correct for instance excessive budget deficits and/or promote fiscal consolidation, to avoid mortgaging future generations… High unemployment and rising social inequalities are the result of the problems that built up before the crisis – debt accumulation, financial market instability, falling demand, etc. Programmes agreed by ministers are meant to remedy this. Of course, these are difficult decisions that involve painful choices and the need to find a balanced and comprehensive mix based on fiscal consolidation, structural reform and smart investments.

In the absence of straight and transparent political communication, we are just sustaining the confusion, perpetuating the impression that we do not believe in these decisions, that there were some other better options that we didn't take or consider – and we are thereby automatically decreasing the support of citizens not only for these decisions but also for the EU as a whole. It's important to realise that national leaders are European leaders too. They bear a dual responsibility. Citizens will always have as a reference point their national government and the national media will always be first and foremost focused on national issues. How national leaders convey the message on EU developments to national media is of crucial importance.

Now where I agree – notably with the European Parliament – is that more democratic accountability is needed on the programmes in general and the work of the troika in particular. As mentioned on several occasions by my colleague Olli Rehn, the troika was created under extreme political and market pressure to prevent a collapse of the euro – and even of the EU, but the governance accountability mechanism can and should still be improved. We need to find ways to discuss with the European Parliament and national parliaments the difficult choices to be made to rebuild our economies.

## The European and national parliaments

As a general proposition the European Parliament's role needs to be reinforced. In relation to European economic governance, it must have the powers to act by helping shape strategic priorities and key recommendations. And reinforcement of the powers of the European and national parliaments must go hand in hand. This should be a rule of thumb: *democratic control must be exercised not only where decisions are taken but also where they have an impact.*

It sounds complicated but it is relatively simple. When we deal with the EU strategic orientations (e.g. the annual growth survey), the European Parliament should be consulted. I am sure that debate on this issue in national parliaments would also be helpful, since it should be a starting point for discussing their national reform programmes with their respective national governments. When the Commission adopts an opinion on a draft national budget, the national parliament should be able to hear it from the Commission.

So we need to step up dialogue with national parliaments on the annual growth survey and country specific recommendations so that they can feed in their views in due course. Before they adopt their national budget, each national parliament should also be given the opportunity to hear a Commissioner on the opinion adopted by the College on the first draft.

Let me stress one point which can be a source of confusion: although the Commission can be heard by both the European and national parliaments it remains formally accountable to the former, which can dismiss it. But in turn, the systematic consultation of national parliaments and the hearings of the Commission by these assemblies will allow them to hold their own governments to account for decisions taken by them in Brussels and in their capitals. This reinforced accountability chain can only be a good thing for democracy.

The dialogue should not be restricted to economic governance, of course. EU legislation concerns all areas of life. As a matter of fact, many of my fellow Commissioners already participate actively in hearings in national parliaments. They are often more than ready to go to their and other national parliaments and engage on behalf of the Commission. But sometimes – and I say 'sometimes' because this has become less the case towards the end of my mandate – we see less appetite for this on the part of some national parliaments. In addition, contacts and interest are often limited to the EU committees of national assemblies. This is clearly a shortcoming. The EU agenda goes well beyond that of EU coordination, into the realms of national transport, energy, telecommunications policy – to name but a few. If a national parliament is willing to discuss the EU railway package the dialogue should take place in the framework of its transport parliamentary committee… not the EU committee; if it is to deal with economic governance, then the finance or economic committee is definitely the most suitable forum. Since the EU covers nearly all aspects of legislation and citizens' lives it should involve all relevant sectorial lead parliamentary committees. This would mirror the way the

European Parliament is organised. And it could provide a basis for strengthened sectorially based inter-parliamentary cooperation between European and national parliaments.

In regard to visibility, I would also advocate, along the lines of what was once proposed to me by Seán Barrett, the Speaker of the Irish House of Representatives, that we organise a dedicated day in the year – Europe Parliamentary Day – when the College members (all my colleagues) would go back to their respective national parliaments and discuss with their national and European elected representatives the challenges facing the EU and the top priorities for citizens. This annual day would provide an EU-wide debate between EU leaders and national representatives on EU issues, with citizens' involvement.

Ultimately a reinforced political dialogue with the Commission and inter-parliamentary cooperation should provide national parliaments with effective tools to improve their capacity to scrutinise, influence and make their national governments accountable for the positions taken at EU level. This should encourage national parliaments to hold their governments more directly accountable for what is being discussed in Brussels, looking at both the substance and subsidiarity issues. National parliaments should in particular be involved upstream in the discussion of reform programmes with their governments, preferably before the programmes are discussed in Brussels. This would have an impact on the flow of information back and forth (between governments and national parliaments), and the organisation of ministerial hearings organised prior (and subsequent) to their participation in Council meetings

I have put a lot of stress on national parliaments for they are key – together with the European Parliament, European political parties and national governments – to bridging the gap with citizens and ensuring democratic scrutiny.

# 5. HOW TO CEMENT OUR ECONOMIES FURTHER? THE MAIN SOURCES OF GROWTH AND JOBS

## First: some much needed 'EU-boosting'

The way the EU sees itself is often self-defeating. We Europeans have a tendency to self-flagellation. And this habit has very deep roots. We see and even overstate our flaws, shortcomings and divisions but aren't good at highlighting what it is that unites us and produces success. We do not know how to 'sell' ourselves. It's almost against our culture – and it can be frustrating at times to see how we can be so down on our own system in the face of so many achievements. Plus it certainly doesn't help in times of hardship.

As I said recently to students at Uppsala University, a fully modern and transformed Europe has nothing to fear from anyone; rather *it should be an example of what other nations should aspire to be*: the safest, fairest, cleanest and greenest place on the planet.

So why can't we see it? We lack confidence. We lack perspective. To regain confidence we have to take a good look at the EU as seen from the outside.

Our external partners never understand our habit of running ourselves down. Quite the opposite: many of them look up to us for the rights and benefits we enjoy, and for the values we cherish. And they see very clearly that what binds us is actually much stronger that what we think divides us.

It has always struck me when travelling or living outside the EU that we are considered a model by many regional groupings (Mercosur in South America, Asean in South-East Asia or the African Union). Many of our competitors would gladly swap positions with us.

How come? Let me expand, by recalling some basic facts that we unfortunately tend to forget and that are quite simply, 'ego' (or should I say 'EU') boosting.

Most EU countries are too small to compete effectively on the global stage. Thanks to the single market we can all do just that, bringing economic growth, lower prices, better services, competition and greater clout on the international stage. Thanks to the single market, the EU has become the world's biggest market economy, accounting for 20% of the global economy, as opposed to 18% for the US. We remain the most important trading bloc, with a share of global trade remaining above 16% while the US has fallen below 14% and China is reaching 12%. Europe is also the preferred place for investment and the world's largest investor abroad. The latest list of the most competitive countries from the World Economic Forum shows that five of the top ten most competitive nations in the world are in the EU – and some are more competitive even than our leading trading partners such as the US, Japan and China. Finally, with around €55 billion spend in official development assistance (ODA) annually the EU, and its Member States, is the world's largest development aid donor. This represents half of global aid. Thanks to EU aid, around 14 million children are going to school, 70 million households have access to water, and over 7.5 million births have been attended by skilled health personnel. 122 million people have been provided emergency relief in over 90 countries outside the EU. This is no mean achievement.

And of course, for nearly 60 years the EU has built its prosperity and integration on a community of values which has brought peace, freedom, security and the highest respect for human rights to our continent. *Let's not forget where we started from.* The EU as we now know it was forged in the fires of world war, born from a world dominated and destroyed by hatred, extreme nationalism, fascism, xenophobia, and anti-semitism. This may perhaps seem obvious. However, as was evidenced by the awarding of the 2012 Nobel Peace Prize to the EU, it has been an exceptional achievement in the history of our old continent, marred by centuries of wars. The last sixty years since the creation of what is now the EU have been the longest period of peace that our continent has ever known – an era in which debates and negotiations around the same table, now with 28 Member State governments (and 751 European parliamentarians!), and respect for the rule of law have replaced war.

I am disappointed when I hear that the so-called 'peace argument' in favour of the EU is simply out-dated, and especially that young people cannot relate to this key reason for which the EU was created in the first place. *I think we should stand back a bit, and look at what's happening around us – still today and not far from the EU.* Just next door actually. We should look at what is taking place in the South, with thousands of people desperately fleeing and trying to cross the Mediterranean in search of a better future, trying to reach EU shores. We should look at Syria with its hundreds of thousands of refugees, and with an end to civil war far from sight. We should look at our eastern borders: for many months we lived through news of the upheavals in Ukraine where its citizens were denied the government they wanted. We saw people waving the European flag in freezing temperatures, day and night. We saw scenes of police shooting citizens, scenes that have become unimaginable in any of today's EU capitals. It took more than three months of sustained protests and bloodshed for the authorities to realise that citizens would not give up on their fight for freedom.

Peace and democracy are so embedded in EU culture that we

take them for granted, forgetting that our neighbours have to fight hard for them. We should look at ourselves with this perspective to realise how fortunate we are and how big an achievement this is.

We are celebrating this year the tenth anniversary of the biggest enlargement of the EU, which brought together the family of countries of Eastern and Western Europe. Joining the EU secured freedom, democracy, protection of human rights and minorities and the rule of law in the Eastern countries, in the same way as it did for Greece, Portugal and Spain twenty years earlier. Since 1993 we are all EU citizens, in addition to national ones. The resulting right to live, travel, work, retire etc. in any EU Member State is an immense benefit which carries a particular significance for those citizens who – like me – were trapped behind the Iron Curtain for more than 40 years.

Where I used to live, in Bratislava, we were actually just a few kilometres away from the real barbed wire fence and border control guard-dogs. And we lived with a very clear idea that we would never be able to cross this river and go behind this fence. So, for the people of my generation (and my elders), for the people who had been confined behind the Iron Curtain, to live in a united Europe, with free and open borders, to be able to travel around the Eurozone with same currency, really is a dream come true… We used to tell the story of the father and son walking along this fence: the son, a child, saw that on the other side there were lights and cars moving and he asked: 'daddy who is behind those bars?'. 'We are, my son' was the father's response. Well, that is exactly how we felt, and very acutely so. I recall what an impact the restrictions on our freedom of speech, reading, expression, had on young people such as I was then. To listen to 'free' music or watch television we had to clandestinely try and catch Austrian media. On the radio, to get the real information about our own country we had to secretly listen to the 'Free Europe' or 'Voice of America' stations, which were jammed by the authorities... Our children take all this freedom for granted, thankfully.

Now, looking at our place in the world: the EU's much envied peace, prosperity and enterprise makes it an economic, standard-setting and civilian power. When it comes to setting standards, for example, we are leading the global battle against climate change, with an ambitious agenda – proposing new targets for cutting EU greenhouse gases by 40% and boosting the share of renewable energies to 27% by 2030.

The success of our integration is not only of vital importance to EU citizens, but also to the world at large. We are China's leading trading partner, they are our second. The EU and US are each other's No. 1 trading partners, with €800 billion in goods and services crossing the Atlantic each year. Many other international partners have a vested interest in our economies performing well.

Our platform for the rest of the 21st century is much stronger than we often think. But it does not guarantee our future. Our risk of decline is real. We need to give a new impetus to the EU economy. We need to invest in the future by building upon the foundations of a sustainable job-rich growth strategy. As far as our integrated economy is concerned we need to give ourselves the means to exploit all available sources of growth and jobs, tapping into the full potential of:

1. Our global trade agenda, with a special focus on our transatlantic partnership;

2. The single market, which needs to be completed;

3. The EU's modern industrial base and capacity for innovation, adjusting education and training to the real needs of industry;

4. Smart regulation and further cutting of red tape.

I describe our 'engines of growth' in what follows.

## 1. Our global trade agenda and the transatlantic trade and investment partnership (TTIP) – a game changer

As mentioned above, the EU managed to keep its share (above 16%) of world trade while the US and Japan lost market share. But where do we go from here?

Global trade is an important engine of growth, one of the main drivers for our industry's competitiveness. Over 25 million people working in the EU have jobs supported by the exports of goods and services to the rest of the world. This number has tripled in the last twenty years.

Since multilateral negotiations (within the World Trade Organisation, WTO) are going slowly, the EU has accelerated negotiation of an array of free trade agreements with key partners. These include Canada, Japan, China, Asean (South-East Asia), India and Mercosur (Brazil, Argentina, Paraguay, Uruguay, Venezuela, Bolivia). Agreements have already been signed with Central American countries, Colombia, Peru, Mexico, South Korea, Singapore and South Africa.

But nothing compares to the potential of our relations with the US. Under the leadership of my colleague Karel de Gucht, we have launched negotiations on the so-called transatlantic trade and investment partnership (TTIP) and if successful this could become a real game changer, creating the largest economic zone in the world. The EU and US between them account for around half the world's economy, a third of all trade flows, and two thirds of world trade in financial services. The total US investment in the EU is five times higher than in all of Asia. Conversely, EU investment in the US is around ten times that of the EU in India and China together. It is estimated that an ambitious and comprehensive transatlantic trade and investment partnership would boost the EU economy by as much as €120 billion a year!

The gains would come from cutting red tape and better coordination between regulators on both sides of the Atlantic, not primarily from removing tariffs, which are already low.

Practical examples of this would be:

– Both the EU and US have high car safety standards. By recognising each other's standards, the TTIP could make it possible for cars proven safe in the EU to be sold in the US without passing further tests – and vice-versa;
– Opening up US government tendering to European construction firms could enable them to compete for big construction and public transport projects;
– Removing barriers to trade, like the US ban on food such as European apples or cheeses;
– A transatlantic free trade area would allow for substantially reducing the gas price gap that prejudices our industry.

The challenge is to open markets, while keeping our high level of regulatory protection in the environmental, health, safety, social and consumer protection fields. We need to make sure that our standards aren't compromised and that there is no 'race to the bottom'. Quite the opposite: our race in this area *must be to the top* – and that will definitely not be easy. Equally important will be the need to find a solution to the conflict settlement system which raises concern for citizens and consumers.

If we can achieve all this, companies will save millions of euros and be able to create hundreds of thousands of jobs. These savings will benefit not only big multinationals, but also our EU SMEs, which bear a higher proportion of regulatory costs (every product, no matter who makes it, has to comply with the same regulatory requirements). This will enable them to substantially reduce the cost of doing business, and to explore new market opportunities. It will also benefit consumers who will be offered a greater choice of high quality and low price products.

Now, returning to the issue of standards: we could create a situation where the shared or mutually accepted EU/US standards became *global* standards thanks to our combined economic weight. This is not just a matter of technical standards but also of social and environmental standards.

We should therefore see the EU-US integrated partnership as a platform or a laboratory for solutions to be applied at the international (WTO) level, especially as they will already be in force in almost half the world's economy. This partnership could also help create conditions for emerging powers to develop social and environmental norms in their production activities.

Reaffirming the transatlantic relationship in this way isn't only about trade and industry's competitiveness: it is also about geopolitical and societal challenges. This is 'soft power': the power to co-opt and convince, to persuade and take others on board with us.

For this ambitious partnership to deliver, we need political courage on both sides of the Atlantic. And when I say *we*, I mean *all of us* – not just the politicians or negotiators on both sides, but everyone involved in its implementation. This includes regulators, parliamentarians, business, chambers of commerce, NGOs, civic groups, trade unions, farmers, think tanks, academia, and more.

## 2. Completion of the single market

The single market is at the heart of European integration. It has brought tangible benefits to citizens and businesses in their daily lives, such as the freedom to buy, sell, live, work, study and travel across Europe. EU citizens like me, whose countries joined the EU in 2004 or later and had previously lived with severe restrictions in these areas, know how priceless this is.

The single market has also driven growth and jobs across the EU. Trade between EU countries grew from €800 billion in 1992 to €2.8 trillion in 2011, while EU trade with the rest of the world tripled, from €500 billion in 1992 to €1.5 trillion in 2011. The single market has stimulated growth and helped create millions of jobs: from 1992 to 2008 it created an extra 2.8 million jobs and an additional 2.1% in gross domestic product (GDP).

But the single market is still incomplete. To further boost our competitiveness we desperately need to remove the outstanding barriers which are hampering growth and preventing us from reaping all the benefits of the internal market. Member States and EU institutions must work together to make sure that our market of 500 million citizens and 23 million companies delivers growth, jobs and renewed confidence in the economy.

To complete the internal market, the European Commission has proposed two packages of proposals – the Single Market Acts I and II (with respectively 12 key actions).

Some substantial progress has already been achieved thanks to the determination of my colleague Michel Barnier. We have simplified public procurement rules and improved the recognition of professional qualifications. We have also managed to reach agreement on a European unitary patent – after 30 years of negotiations! – which will cut substantially (by a factor of seven, and some even say ten) the cost of innovating.

But we need to do more, undoubtedly. Let me give you some examples.

## Developing further integrated networks

There is still a lot to be done to make the single market work better for services, which represent 70% of our economy, and network industries (energy, transport and telecoms). Markets are still fragmented with suboptimal size companies operating in small markets and insufficient EU-wide infrastructure.

Services and network industries both have a huge untapped growth and employment potential.

## Fostering mobility of citizens and businesses across borders

We need to help people look for jobs in other EU countries. Despite the economic crisis, two million vacancies in the EU remain unfilled!

We also need to create new finance vehicles to make it easier for people to invest in long-term projects, modernising insolvency rules to facilitate cross-border procedures and ultimately helping businesses survive (or offering entrepreneurs a second chance).

All this requires measures to be adopted at EU level and implemented by Member States.

One of the concrete measures proposed by the Commission and still to be fully implemented on the ground is the EU 'blue card' – the EU-wide work permit granting highly skilled non-EU citizens a series of rights (including on working conditions, mobility between Member States and family reunification rules) for a maximum period of four years, with the possibility of renewal. This should allow us to meet skills shortages that cannot be filled by EU nationals.

## Supporting the digital economy

A digital single market offers a competitive advantage that we must develop. It is a real driver for growth and competitiveness. It also creates virtually new jobs such as community managers, web architects, etc.

E-commerce is a key aspect and implementing more efficient payment systems will play an important part in this. To support the digital single market we must ensure that as many people and businesses as possible are able to use high-speed communications. We need to harness big data to the benefit of citizens, public authorities and private companies. We also need to promote electronic invoicing for public procurement. Cross-border recognition and verification of e-signatures and identities is also key to the digital single market.

## Strengthening social entrepreneurship, cohesion and consumer confidence

We need to adopt rules on the safety of products and their enforcement. We must also ensure that all EU citizens have access to a bank account, that bank charges are transparent, and that it's easier for people to switch banks… these are just a few examples.

Member States' transposition of single market legislation is vital. We need to help with the correct transposition and application of EU law – and to continue looking at the implementation as part of the European semester. This means going beyond pure legal transposition. Member States should discuss the *opportunities – not just the constraints* – relating to single market implementation. This debate should take place at national level, with policy makers taking an active part. To be able to make good use of the opportunities provided by the single market, citizens and businesses must be made aware of their rights and how to exercise them.

## 3. A reinforced EU industrial base and innovation capacity

The EU is a world leader in many strategic manufacturing industries such as the automotive sector, aeronautics, telecommunications, engineering, space, chemicals, cosmetics and pharmaceuticals. Industry accounts for over four-fifths of EU exports and 80% of private sector research and innovation. EU competitiveness is highly dependent on prioritising investment in industry, as it is a major source of growth, job creation, and innovation.

However, the EU's industrial base is in decline. This is a fact. While some sectors of the economy show signs of recovery, more than 3.5 million jobs in manufacturing industry have been lost since 2008, and its share of EU GDP has dropped to about 15.1%. In comparison, in the 1990s, EU manufacturing industry contributed 20% of our GDP. Moreover, since 1995, our productivity has grown less than that of Japan and the US. Aided by lower transport and communication costs, industrial operations have increasingly been sliced up into complex packages, which are geographically dispersed and with production sites often being moved closer to customers in emerging markets. Meanwhile, investment in research and innovation is just 2.06% of GDP for the whole EU, well below the target of 3%, which holds back the modernisation of our industrial base.

EU companies are also burdened by much higher energy costs than most of their leading competitors, most notably the US and China. They also experience difficulties finding skilled labour, especially in the fields of science, technology, engineering and mathematics. Finally, the EU's capacity to attract finance, in particular for SMEs, has deteriorated, notably in the South of Europe. Only half of the small businesses who need credit in Spain get the amount they need – and only a third in Greece.

In its 10 October 2012 Communication *A Stronger European Industry for Growth and Economic Recovery* the European Commission stated the aim to increase industry's share of GDP to 20% by 2020.

*This has to be a priority.* We need to revitalise EU industry with the aim of delivering sustainable growth and creating high value jobs. We need to turn the know-how of our researchers and companies into marketable and innovative high value-added products and applications. We need to make the EU more attractive to foreign researchers and entrepreneurs from all over the world, capitalising on our values, lifestyle and the quality of our workforce and efficiency of our public services.

More precisely, how can we do this?

Here are some priority actions, building upon (and beyond) what the Commission is currently putting in place. What we have romantically called a 'European Industrial Renaissance'.

We need:

– To focus our investment in *targeted new technologies* – the technologies of tomorrow – to improve the business environment, maintain our leadership in key industries, and develop a sustainable green economy. Our economies were transformed by technologies such as air travel and telecommunications. Some other key enabling technologies have been identified by my colleague Antonio Tajani as needing greater support at EU level: bio-technologies, micro and nano-electronics, advanced materials and industrial biotech… these technologies offer solutions to the problems we face in our everyday lives, to help find treatments for diseases, cut $CO_2$ emissions and other sources of urban pollution, develop alternative sources of energy and ways of recycling waste, improve the quality of our water supply and the food we eat…

- To explore and develop *innovative financing instruments*. To this end, we should build upon the experience acquired by the European Investment Bank (EIB, described as 'the world's largest public financial or lending institution') to further develop and implement project bonds (or loans), in cooperation with the European Commission. Project bonds aim at stimulating capital market financing for big infrastructure projects in transport, energy and ICT.

- To make sure *public-private co-financing* is further developed. In Horizon 2020, the research and innovation framework programme adopted for the current seven years, the Commission is joining forces with the private sector through public-private partnerships in key areas of industry to help stimulate innovation. EU policies must continue to be successful in leveraging private funds so as to promote research and innovation and foster partnerships between the private and public sectors. Good collaboration between the research community and business as well as social organisations is central to creating innovation – i.e. to making sure that we create value or downstream economic impacts via the introduction of new products, processes, services and ways of doing things.

– To zoom in on *smart specialisation to enable regions to focus on innovation* through partnerships involving businesses, public entities and knowledge institutions. Over the next seven years at least €100 billion of European funds is being made available to regions to support these efforts.

– To ensure better *access to markets and finance*, through an effective system of lending to the real economy and pan-European venture capital markets. This is particularly important for SMEs.

– To ensure that *skills match industry's needs*. Cooperation between education, research, training and business must be strengthened to that end. We must also prioritise the development of apprenticeships.

– To make sure we have the *right regulatory framework* for investment in innovation by cutting red tape, making our own regulations more business friendly, and promoting entrepreneurship.

– To *dismantle barriers* that hamper the internal market as mentioned before, most notably in the network industries: transport, digital communications and energy.

– To conclude *bilateral trade agreements* with key partners – most notably the US – and promote international standards. This could become a game changer for EU industry, as argued above.

As I said earlier, in launching any new policy, programme or project we must always carefully assess the impact it will have on growth and jobs. What will it do for employment? What will be the social consequences?

On the Commission side, our prime responsibility is to ensure that all policies take into account the objective of developing EU industry's competitiveness. This includes policies on trade, energy, intellectual property, research and innovation and competition, as well as monetary policy. We also have to ensure that EU funds are targeted at igniting growth and employment by acting as leverage for research, innovation and industrial competitiveness.

We can also play a more active role in facilitating negotiations between targeted companies, trade unions and relevant national, regional and local administrations to avoid plant closures and massive layoffs in the EU. This has started, but should intensify.

Finally, we should engage more forcefully in developing our economic networks and economic diplomacy in close partnership with the Member States. In general, EU industrial policy can only deliver if it involves all the relevant forces in the economy, including large and small enterprises, trade unions and employers' organisations, the banking sector, health and education, public laboratories and private sector R&D, universities, the EU, national, regional and local administrations, competitiveness clusters and business incubators. We need to build strong innovation partnerships and industrial alliances. We already have some EU success stories. Our strong partnerships with Airbus and Ariane in the aerospace industry should serve as a benchmark. It is a matter of working together, with a view to making our industry more competitive and innovative.

## 4. Smart regulation and cutting red tape

As I described in chapter 2, the meetings of the General Affairs Council (GAC) deal with politically sensitive issues and are sometimes intense; emotions can rise high... and on such occasions, humour helps ease the tension. And we do have some very humorous moments. I recall a recent exchange with the Dutch Europe Minister, Frans Timmermans, who is well known for striving to cut red tape. In reference to the complexities of EU law, Frans paraphrased Emperor Joseph II who had allegedly complained to Mozart that his opera *Abduction from the*

*Seraglio* was '*too fine for my ears – there are too many notes*'. It was Frans's polite way of suggesting that the EU institutions were too often prone to regulatory overzealousness. With the help of my adviser, I was fortunate to be able to offer the response that Mozart dared give his Emperor: '*there are just as many notes as there should be, your imperial Highness*'. This cleared the air in the Council room, and allowed us to have a lively and interesting discussion as to how many notes there should be… because a bit of legislation that may seem a useless embellishment to one Member State, may sometimes appear indispensable to another.

## Smart regulation and subsidiarity

We now have one of the most open and transparent policy processes in the world, with impact assessments and public consultations on legislative proposals being employed to take on board the widest possible range of views and ensure that new legislation improves upon the old.

This extensive preparatory work means that we only make proposals where they are really needed, in compliance with the principles of subsidiarity and proportionality. These principles are at the heart of our approach to regulation and guide our work. The question of whether we should propose action at EU level, and if so how, is examined in green papers, white papers, policy communications, and extensive public consultations. Our roadmaps for all major EU initiatives include a fuller analysis of subsidiarity and proportionality issues – which also involves a consultation of all interested parties. The subsidiarity assessment is verified by the Impact Assessment Board, which often suggests improvements to be followed. Finally, as explained above, our proposals and the subsidiarity justification are now scrutinised by all national parliaments, which can ask the Commission to revise its 'homework'. It is rather reassuring that in the four years since this latter control has been in force, only two proposals have been the subject of 'yellow cards' from the national parliaments and none have been the subject of 'orange cards'.

What is certain is that the added value of acting at EU level ought to be demonstrated right from the start, the regulatory framework rendered stable and understandable and administrative burdens and compliance costs reduced to the minimum.

Which does not mean we always get it right. But even if we don't always get it right, we always try our best to. Our objective is to ensure that EU legislation is 'fit for purpose' to put Europe back on track towards more growth and jobs.

## REFIT and SMEs

With this in mind, simplification and the reduction of the overall burden of regulation are key priorities. In other words: reaching our objectives with the lowest possible cost and burden.

The Regulatory Fitness and Performance Programme (REFIT) launched in December 2012 constitutes an important contribution to this objective. REFIT expresses the Commission's commitment to a *simple, clear, stable and predictable* regulatory framework for businesses, workers and citizens. It focuses on efficient and effective legislation and application of the law, with the least regulatory burden. It sets out where the Commission will act to simplify further or withdraw EU legislation, in order to ease the burden on businesses and facilitate implementation.

To this end the Commission has screened the entire stock of EU legislation, paying attention to each phase of the policy cycle (from the impact assessment to *ex post* evaluation). Ten sectors have been prioritised for further evaluation, simplification and reduction of administrative burdens, with a major focus on SMEs. Concrete improvements that are being introduced to help SMEs include, for example, simplified procedures for cross-frontier small claims, exemptions from the use of tachographs in road transport, and in respect of the REACH regulations for the chemicals sector, substantial reductions in fees for SMEs. A standard VAT declaration and procedures to ensure quicker refunds have also been proposed. All in all, REFIT currently covers a total of over 100 actions.

But we are not starting from scratch. Between 2007 and 2012, the original target of reducing the administrative burden for businesses by 25% was achieved and even exceeded. We have now gone beyond the original target by tabling proposals with a total burden reduction potential close to €41 billion (33%).

When we cut red tape at the EU level we do need to make sure that this is implemented at the national level so that it benefits citizens. This is why we're closely monitoring the outcome of these policies.

We need to intensify this work. Businesses, civil society and citizens do not yet feel the impact in everyday life of this cutting of red tape. We must make sure that our policies reach the citizens. To this end we are increasing our monitoring of how reduction in red tape is being implemented on the ground by the Member States. We will now have a scoreboard to track annual progress on their implementation. We are deadly serious about it. For what is at stake is the misleading perception of a Europe that is bogged down by bureaucracy.

If you look at the Commission work programme produced annually, it is now divided into four parts. The last two parts deal solely with, respectively, legislation that needs *updating* and legislation that *we should get rid of*. There is a part wholly devoted to initiatives to improve the efficiency and effectiveness of EU regulation and reducing regulatory burden. I am convinced that this is the model that should be followed by the next Commission.

But whilst it's important to evaluate the impacts, costs and burdens of EU action, it's equally important to assess the 'cost of non-Europe'. How much will it costs citizens and businesses if we don't propose one common set of rules at EU level?

On the question of simplification, I am often told by British ministers that the Commission should embrace the approach: 'bring one (EU law) in, take one out'. I have a response to that: '*let's bring one EU law in and take 28 national laws out!*' That would be a good start.

Let me give you a telling example of what can be done, the fourth railway package...

## The fourth railway package

Replacing legislation in 28 Member States with one law can add value and simplify life for businesses and consumers alike. The latest (fourth) railway package from my colleague Siim Kallas is a good example of this. This package aims to replace over 11,000 different rules and standards in effect across Europe today with one sensible piece of legislation.

This harmonised set of rules at EU level will significantly reduce the cost and the time it takes to authorise rolling stock. Currently, for example, authorising a new locomotive to operate in a single country can cost up to €6 million. Costs increase significantly when the procedure needs to be repeated in several countries and these procedures can take up to two years! Currently rail authorisations and safety certificates are issued by each Member State. This clearly hinders the effective operation of the single market. Under the new proposals, the European Rail Agency will become a 'one stop shop' issuing EU-wide authorisations for suppliers and EU-wide safety certificates for operators. Simplification at its best…

# 6. TOWARDS A COMMON FOREIGN AND SECURITY POLICY (CFSP)?

Numerous books have been written on the external relations of the EU and its foreign and security policy, so I'll only provide a brief glimpse of my personal experience and related thoughts on this important topic.

The EU is perceived as a strong economic bloc but not as a global political player. Yet this is often a wrong perception.

One thing is for sure: we could still learn from our American friends when it comes to communication. The EU Humanitarian Office (ECHO) is almost systematically the first on the ground providing relief and emergency assistance to vulnerable populations in trouble spots and disaster areas. Faster than the Japanese themselves in the case of the tsunami, for instance. But this is overshadowed by the sight of big US planes landing, with a large international press corps accompanying them, and naturally capturing all the media attention as a result!

We lack some communication skills and maybe that also goes back to what I had to say before: we work incredibly hard to help millions of people but we do not take sufficient pride in our many achievements…

## A world in turmoil

The world around us is changing profoundly. The geopolitical and competitive landscape is rapidly evolving.

The United States, our traditional ally, has clearly shown in recent years that while it wishes to maintain its strong links with the EU, it does so in the context of geopolitical repositioning and an increasing focus on other regions of the world.

Emerging economies – especially the 'BRICS' (Brazil, Russia, India, China and South Africa), first amongst which is China – are developing their own, and in some cases impressive, strategic and diplomatic skills and resources on the world stage. We are also slowly moving towards a less unilateral monetary system, and the dollar's hegemonic status is slowly but surely losing ground.

Some emerging powers (China, India, Russia, Brazil) are literally 'continent-countries'. At this pace, in a few decades – or even before – no single EU country, except perhaps Germany – will be sitting around the G8 table. Only the combined power of all EU Member States will be certain to give us a permanent seat there. Again, the cost of non-Europe is what we should bear in mind…

In this context, the EU is at a make or break point. If we miss the boat, we – the EU – will slowly but surely fall into oblivion. So how do we convert the economic giant that we are today into a fully fledged foreign policy actor?

## What we need is the will!

*We need the will to use the instruments provided by the Lisbon Treaty.*
We now have a diplomatic service in place: the European External Action Service (EEAS). In the lead-up to the Lisbon Treaty there were high hopes linked to the creation of the EEAS. It was expected that Europe would acquire its own European diplo-

matic corps, which would match those of the big Member States' 12,000-15,000 strong diplomatic resources.

I worked hard, together with Catherine Ashton (representing the EEAS), Miguel Ángel Moratinos (representing the Council), Guy Verhofstadt, Elmar Brok and Roberto Gualtieri (for the European Parliament) to create this service from scratch. During the negotiations we felt how important it was for national ministers to have the European foreign and security policy and the work of the EEAS under their close scrutiny, which is rather understandable. We encountered limitations, therefore, ranging from the budget to the size, composition, number of personnel and decision-making process. In the end we brokered a deal, and thanks to Catherine Ashton's determination, progress has been achieved on the ground. The EEAS is working. The EU is now represented in more than 130 countries through its delegations. Initial tensions are subsiding. Cooperation is starting to kick in. We now need to consolidate our strategic relations with key partners.

And in the last year, under the leadership of the High Representative, we have been starting to achieve some breakthroughs. I refer to the agreement between Serbia and Kosovo (also thanks to the intensive work of my colleague Štefan Füle) or that on the Iran nuclear programme where the High Representative negotiated intensively on behalf of the E3 (UK, France and Germany) +3 (US, Russia and China).

Time is needed for the EEAS and CFSP to succeed, but it is of paramount importance that the EU foreign affairs ministers see it as their own service. It must become a platform which enables the individual Member States to dramatically increase their political weight through collective action. Foreign ministers need to put their hearts into creating a common policy. And they must be ready to pool more of their competences to win back some of the lost prestige they once had as individual nation-states.

The Member States should not send out the presidents of the

European Council and European Commission with firm positions on matters such as human rights, copyright and the environment, while in parallel undermining them by seeking bilateral contacts with countries such as China for national advantage. We are creating the conditions of a division. We should have one line and respect it. This dual approach is detrimental to everyone in the long run.

It is of course only natural that government leaders will continue to seek personal and national political benefits from a big new initiative; and, in particular, where matters of war and peace are involved, major decisions relating to the use of the armed forces will always remain within the national realm. But there are foreign policy areas and strategies where EU/Member State cooperation *must* improve if the EU as a whole and Member States in particular want to remain active players.

The logic of cooperation should apply to all external policy fields, for they are inextricably linked. I agree with the call from several foreign ministers that more coordination is needed inside the Commission and with the EEAS, between foreign and security policy and trade, development aid, humanitarian assistance, environmental policy, the external dimension of energy policy, etc.

## A common EU defence policy

National defence budgets are shrinking while the cost of major defence systems rises continuously. And our defence market is fragmented. We invest separately. We lack coordination at EU level. The challenge is both political and economic.

*Political*: regional conflicts are not bound to cease. We have had ample proof of this in the South (e.g. Libya, Mali) and the East (Georgia, Ukraine). And US engagement can no longer be taken for granted. What is at stake is our ability to act rapidly in crisis situations – our capacity to deploy autonomous military capabilities.

*Economic*: we need to build a strong industrial defence market. The only way to produce synergies and economies of scale is to work together, to share resources and competitive advantages. To this end, a common procurement policy is key. Reinforced cooperation and consolidation of our defence industry is also about promoting jobs and technological innovation in such sectors as space, aeronautics, energy, cyber, maritime surveillance, communications, data collection, access, transmission, storage, etc.

## One phone number to call Europe? A false question (*with all due respect to its author*)

Henry Kissinger, when US Secretary of State, is famously said to have asked: 'who do I call if I want to call Europe?'

Things have changed quite dramatically since those days. We now have a High Representative (who is also a Commission Vice-President) in charge of both CFSP and the coordination of external relations. However, while there is now certainly one number that can be called, that does not mean it is the *only* one. We have – and need – the Commission President to deal with things at his level in relation to the outside world; the President of the European Council likewise represents the European Union in foreign and security policy at his level (working hand in hand with the Commission President); and in addition we also have a Trade Commissioner dealing with international commerce, a Development Commissioner, and a Commissioner for Humanitarian Aid. And each Member State also has its own foreign, trade, and development ministers...

*But is this really very different from the US?* Is the American external relations portfolio actually the preserve of a single person or body? Depending on the issue at hand – and on who is calling! – one may need to contact the US President, his National Security Adviser, the Vice-President, the Secretary of State, the Secretary of Defence, the Secretary of Commerce or the head of a federal agency, not to mention the international role of the US Senate (e.g. the Chair of its Foreign Affairs Committee), and so on. At the end of the day, the important thing is to know whom to contact and for what. External powers do not experience any greater difficulties in dealing with the EU than they do with their other partners. Quite the contrary: they tend to benefit from our tradition of working in close cooperation (e.g. the Presidents of the European Council and the Commission, along with the relevant Heads of State or Government, when it comes to the G20/G8) and from maximising the effectiveness of our representation by early preparation and coordination.

# 7. A POSITIVE AGENDA FOR THE EU

## 'Big on big things and smaller on smaller things'

As President Barroso put it in his 2013 State of the Union address, when it comes to generating growth and jobs 'the EU needs to be big on big things and smaller on smaller things'. It means that the Commission seeks integration in priority areas (e.g. the banking union) but it should not meddle in everything. We need to have clear positive and negative priorities. This shows the pragmatic approach of the Commission whereby subsidiarity and proportionality are key concepts in providing legitimacy to EU action.

As for *negative* priorities, the EU needs to refrain from acting where there is no proven added value. We should be courageous and not hesitate to say 'no' whenever justified: to farmers, if they want to regulate on cucumbers, or to hairdressers on their working conditions, or to olive oil producers over the use of small bottles in restaurants, etc. This also goes for specific requests from Member States. Our subsidiarity check must lead us to openly refuse to act. Our credibility depends on it.

## The EU and the challenge of globalisation

Globalisation brings its share of opportunities and concerns. It forces everyone to compete on a global scale – from big multinationals to SMEs, even students. And it will not go away. It is here to stay. Of course there are plenty of direct benefits – for example, in terms of cheaper airfares, more keenly priced products, and easy access to information – but at the same time we are legitimately concerned about the way these internationally-traded products are made; concerned about the disrespect for environmental standards by some manufacturers; concerned to see factories collapsing in Bangladesh, the social or employment conditions of children in some Asian or African countries, and so forth. How do we respond? Do we restore borders, quotas, excise duties?

We know this is not the cure. As explained in chapter 5, the EU is in a very good starting position to shape globalisation. We need to exercise our global clout – our 'soft power', with a forceful and positive agenda relating not only to our economy but also to our living standards, our education systems, our values, our drive to empower women, to promote development and the protection of high environmental and social standards. These are key elements for us to shape the globalisation process and make that process a more 'European' one, a world that is fairer, greener, cleaner, safer, more respectful of human rights, labour codes, and generally more sustainable.

The challenge of globalisation is therefore what has to shape our *positive* agenda or priorities at EU level. And I emphasise at EU level – or via EU leverage – for there are areas where the level of a Member State is simply not sufficient to seize the challenges of today's interdependent economies, such as in external trade, competition, the internal market, innovation, research and development. The EU must intervene to provide a level playing field that creates opportunities for businesses and citizens, while preserving our high environmental and social standards. For some issues – e.g. climate change, international terrorism – do not stop at our national borders and therefore the EU is the right level of action to address them.

Even when it does seem obvious that the EU should intervene it is never taken for granted. No action is taken at EU level unless there is a clear demonstrated advantage in doing so. Subsidiarity is both a principle of efficiency and democracy, requiring decisions to be taken as efficiently, as openly and as close to our citizens as possible. To the extent that EU-level action is considered necessary, it is important that it is done in the most efficient, transparent, democratic and accountable way possible.

It is our responsibility to make sure that citizens are involved in the shaping of political action at EU level, be it through their government or parliamentary representatives, through the election of the Commission or direct democracy instruments like the European Citizens' Initiative.

## The future is in our hands

Six years after the fall of Lehman Brothers, we may be seeing the light at the end of the tunnel. The economy is moving out of recession, many default countries are back on the markets (with reduced interest rate spreads), a reindustrialisation is being launched, and we have made qualitative progress towards banking, economic and fiscal union.

But the situation is not all rosy: our recovery is still fragile, many people are suffering from the social consequences of the crisis, and the trust of our citizens is at a record-low level. This creates fertile ground for populist and extreme nationalist parties to prosper. As I mentioned right at the start of this book, we need to counter this with formidable energy, for pro-European forces must take the lead in the 2014 debate, and beyond.

The best way to fight populism is to offer pragmatic solutions by focusing on a handful of result-oriented priorities. It is to make sure that EU action does not replace but – quite the opposite – adds value to national action. It is to involve citizens in the shaping of a positive agenda for the EU, so they have a say in building a more efficient and stronger union.

## A three-pillar positive agenda for the EU

Our positive agenda could be based on three main pillars.

*Pillar I. A long-term strategy for growth that is job-rich and sustainable*

To transform the incipient recovery into job-rich sustainable growth, we must:
- unleash all the potential of the single market – working with the Member States to overcome the implementation gap;
- boost our trade agenda and in particular our transatlantic partnership (TTIP);
- incentivise EU Member States' social policies and employment/active labour market reforms – not just fiscal consolidation – through enhanced EU fiscal capacity, monitoring, coordination and support;
- continue modernising and simplifying our business friendly regulatory framework, most notably for SMEs;
- reverse our industrial decline in order to reach the target of 20% of GDP represented by the manufacturing sector by 2020 through an active competitiveness policy and investing massively in research and innovation to leverage private funding at EU level. To that end, efficient public-private partnerships should be developed.

*Pillar II. A fully-fledged 'EU economic government'*

For the first time in the history of the EU, a banking union is being set up with reinforced supervisory powers at EU level. Member States are also coordinating their economic and budgetary policies, with monitoring, reporting and recommendations by the Commission. The huge interdependence between our economies has led to the political realisation that intimate mutual coordination and monitoring of not only each other's fiscal policies but also internal labour markets and social systems is in everyone's interest.

For a qualitative jump to take place from this strengthened model of economic governance to a *genuine economic government at EU level*, we need to go one step further and reinforce the role of both the European and national parliaments.

We also need to develop a genuine fiscal capacity that would allow the Commission to give better support to the much-needed reforms. The right balance needs to be found between (reform-led) responsibility on the one hand and solidarity (in terms of financial support) on the other. In terms of reform, the balance should also be sought between fiscal consolidation to recover margins for manoeuvre and growth-enhancing measures to re-launch the economy.

## *Pillar III. Collective responsibility and ownership of EU decisions*

This relates to the political communication issue that I have already referred to on several occasions. And it starts at home: there are plenty of national politicians who need to stop playing with domestic public opinion, blaming 'Brussels' or other governments for decisions they have themselves agreed to be necessary, such as to bring budget deficits under control. Too often, unpopular decisions are represented by the political elite as being taken against the will of national governments where this is clearly not the case – blaming 'Europe' as if it had nothing to do with them.

And on the other side of the coin, how many times do we see a decision that is popular at home presented as the sole achievement of a national minister, when in reality it emerged from a collective endeavour? Such situations are indeed all too common, with consensus decisions reached in Brussels fragmenting into 28 national 'victories for common sense' by the time an issue reaches the national media. This is what I like to call '*the*

Brusselisation of failure and the nationalisation of success', which has gone a long way towards perpetuating some of the most harmful myths about the EU project. And it ends up sounding as if there is no one really prepared to take responsibility.

For leaders to take individual responsibility for, and accept collective ownership of, decisions we need to build up a joint communication strategy. It is up to both EU and national politicians – they often come from the same breed – to collectively assume responsibility for the decisions they take, and to engage in the debate on the contours or shape of the European project and on the kind of policies that we are seeking to carry through. The accountability chain must go all the way to the people. This is the only way of engaging our fellow citizens and ultimately of building trust in and ownership of EU decisions.

We must also help citizens engage directly. Direct participatory e-democracy should be benchmarked at EU level (with the example of Estonia) and developed to offer citizens the possibility of 'e-shaping' political action …

*A positive EU agenda – three pillars in support of an EU political union*

## EU political union – a target within sight

EU political union is on our horizon. To avoid domestic isola-
tionism, EU fragmentation and decline, we have no other option but to dig deeper into the EU project. Member States and
citizens alike need a powerful Europe. And a powerful Europe
means deeper economic, fiscal, social and ultimately political
integration, with an investment budget that allows us to support much needed reforms at national level, in support of our
growth and competitiveness strategy. A stronger political union
also means enhanced representative and participatory democracy and an EU foreign policy based on a genuine diplomatic
service and a common military defence.

A political union should not be seen as the sort of bureaucratic super-state which is sometimes depicted by Eurosceptics.
I know many citizens fear that a political union would take
away from them their national sovereignty and identity – that
their national flag, their anthem, their language, their national
football team, their customs, cultural traditions and heritage
would disappear. Let me be clear: this is not the Europe we
want. I am convinced that our national flag, our national team,
our hometown, will always be our first bond and there will always be that special feeling that will be preserved. This feeling,
these ties, will be always be preserved through our traditions,
through the education of our children, through our national history and heritage. Europe is a continent of diversity and must
remain so. No one will take this away from us. Citizens will not
allow it. Political leaders will not allow it.

What an EU political union *will* do on the other hand is to
build bridges. Bridges between the EU and its citizens, and between its citizens – most notably between those of the Northern
and the Southern Member States – and between the Eurozone
and the rest of the EU, including the UK.

## The ballot, the street, the internet and the classroom

These are some of today's most important channels for freedom of expression and direct democratic participation.

The ballot – *representative democracy* – is the most traditional one. But we now need to be able to interact with citizens through other means, and political leaders need to offer user-friendly platforms for *participatory democracy* to prosper.

For participation to bear its fruits, political parties and the media, among others, also need to play their respective roles independently and responsibly, that is without veering into uninformed hasty judgments and populism. We need a diversity of viewpoints and well informed citizens who can decide for themselves and take ownership of the EU project.

To this end, I cannot overstate the role of education and schools. Education gives our children the skills to lead their lives as individuals and, as citizens, to shape the society in which they want to live. Potentially all young people should be able to consciously benefit from the realities of the EU in the course of their studies. This applies to the benefits of life-changing learning abroad but also of being offered a genuine curriculum on the EU.

But education about the EU is seldom an integral part of national programmes in schools. All EU countries should offer a pedagogical approach to EU history and values, looking at how the EU functions, how it is organised, what impacts it has, the rights of EU citizens and the like. This should be in addition to, and not a substitute for, national history courses which are bound to remain in the core curricula. But EU studies could be introduced in the same way as civics have been brought into many curricula.

For this to happen we need all Member States on board because education in general and school curricula in particular remain firmly in the hands of our national governments. With strong political impetus and leadership, such programmes could become part and parcel of a new European Education Area, with extended mutual recognition of diplomas, degrees and qualifications. The mainstreaming of 'EU education', as we might call it, should actually not only involve schools (and universities) but also vocational training. Thus, as part of their training, doctors would also get to learn about the European Medicines Agency; automotive manufacturers would hear about how European norms and standards are adopted and applied, and so on. We need to do this for the sake of offering our children and adults education and training that widens their horizons and empowers them to function as active EU citizens, workers, consumers, etc.

For the EU is not just about economics or trade or competition or politics. *It is about sharing a community of values*, about wanting to live, work, and study together and exchanging experiences to build cultural bonds beyond and across borders. It is ultimately about working to build what the founding fathers described in the preamble of the Treaty of Rome as an *'ever closer Union among the peoples of Europe'*.

Building bridges with and between EU citizens – this is certainly the most pressing challenge ahead of us.